101 Life Skills and Tips for Teens

D1521580

Contents

Introduction

Becoming a teenager is incredibly exciting. You have more freedom to choose what direction you want your life to take as you grow older. It's a time to choose what subjects to take in school, decide whether to pursue college after high school, and explore your different career options. You will decide on a career path to pursue, making important decisions, make and review friendships plus take responsibility for your own well-being, including physical and mental health.

Whatever your case, if you are in your teens, this is when you develop yourself, build your strengths, and work on your weaknesses – whether that's learning how to cook or change the oil in your car. Because with great freedom comes great responsibilities - not to mention a TON of new skills you'll need to master as a teenager!

As a teenager you have so many more challenges. You might feel pressure to conform to expectations and deal with peer pressure - but you are a unique individual and you can create your own path in life! You might experience stress, anxiety, and pressure to perform well in school - but there are strategies to help you through any difficult situations. And sometimes as you strive for independence, sometimes conflicts with parents and other family members may arise - but these don't have to last long with the tips in this book!

This is because being a teenager is not easy. It can be super challenging. So it is ok to feel lost and overwhelmed at times. But the good news is that you're in the right place. We're going to cover all your teenager questions like.... How can I succeed in school and prepare for college or a career? What do I want to do with my life? How can I manage my finances and save money? How do I cook something that's both healthy and delicious? And where have all my socks gone?!

In the next pages, all your questions will be answered. You'll learn not only how to survive your teenage years, but how to be a super successful teen too. So let's get started!

Family

As a teenager you are going to rely on your family a lot. These are the people you can go to when everything else feels like it's falling apart. You know, those people who always have your back no matter what?

Our family can give us advice, listen to us when we need to vent, and celebrate our successes with us. And when times are tough, they can be our rock, providing us with that emotional support that we need. Our family also helps us build our confidence and self-esteem, and gives us a sense of belonging.

But it's not just about having someone to lean on, your family can also help shape you into the person you're meant to be. They can help you develop your values and beliefs, and give you a sense of purpose and direction in life. It's always worth taking a moment to appreciate all the love and support they give you.

Families come in all shapes and sizes. For example, you might have a traditional family with a mom, dad, and siblings. But there are also lots of other types of families out there. Maybe you have two moms or two dads, or you live with your grandparents. Some families are blended, meaning they have step-siblings or half-siblings. And some people consider their close friends to be like family. Really, there are so many different types of families, and all of them are valid and important. What is really important is that you have people you can rely on and who love you for who you are, regardless of what your family unit looks like.

Your parents

Life isn't perfect, and we all know that getting along with our parents or guardians can sometimes be a bit of a challenge. I mean, they just don't understand us, right? But the truth is, having a good relationship with our parents is super important. They're the people who love us the most and want what's best for us, even if it doesn't always seem that way. That's why I wanted to share some tips on how we can all get along better with our parents. Trust me, if you follow these tips, you'll be surprised at how much smoother things can go at home. So, let's dive in!

Communicate openly

Effective communication is essential for a good relationship between parents and teenagers. Try to express your feelings and thoughts clearly and calmly to your parents, and listen to their perspectives as well.

Respect your parents

Respect is a two-way street. If you want your parents to respect you, you need to respect them too. Respect their opinions, decisions, and boundaries.

Avoid arguments

It's normal to have disagreements with your parents, but it's important to avoid arguments. Try to keep the conversation civil and respectful. If things start to get heated, stop the conversation, take some time out to cool down and talk about it again later.

Be honest

Honesty is important in any relationship. Be honest with your parents about your feelings, thoughts, and actions. If you make a mistake, be honest, take accountability and try to make things right.

Set boundaries

As a teenager, you are growing up and trying to establish your independence. You'll need to communicate with your parents to gain their trust and ask for help when you need it.

Help around the house

One way to show your parents that you appreciate them is by helping around the house. You could do the dishes, clean your room or take out the trash. Your parents will appreciate this a lot and will be very impressed at how responsible and mature you are becoming.

Spend time together

Hanging out with your family and having fun together is important for building relationships. Find activities that you and your parents enjoy doing together, such as watching a movie or playing a game.

Keep your promises

If you make a promise to your parents, keep it. This will show them that you are trustworthy and reliable.

Show gratitude

Show your parents that you appreciate them. Say thank you and tell them that you love them!

Be patient

It's important to be patient with your parents. They are trying their best to raise you and guide you through life. Remember that they are human and make mistakes too.

Your brothers & sisters

We all love our brothers and sisters. They're family, right? But let's face it, getting along with our brothers and sisters can be tough at times. They know exactly how to push our buttons, and it can feel like we're always fighting or bickering over something. But at the end of the day, our siblings are some of the most important people in our lives. They're the ones who know us better than anyone else and have been there through thick and thin. That's why I wanted to share some tips on how we can all get along better with our siblings. Trust me, if you follow these tips, you'll be surprised at how much more harmonious your home life can be.

Communication is key

Like any relationship, communication is important in getting along with your siblings. Try to talk to them openly and listen to what they have to say.

Respect each other's space

It's important to respect each other's boundaries and personal space. Don't invade their personal space without permission.

Avoid taking things personally

Siblings can sometimes say hurtful things, but it's important not to take everything personally. Remember that they might be going through their own issues and it's not always about you.

Share responsibility

Help each other with household chores and other responsibilities. This can be a great way to bond and work together as a team.

Find common interests

Try to find common interests with your siblings and spend time doing activities you both enjoy. This can help you connect and build a stronger bond.

Be forgiving

Forgiveness is important in any relationship, especially with siblings. Learn to forgive and move on from past disagreements.

Set boundaries

Setting boundaries is important in any relationship, including with siblings. Let them know what you are comfortable with and what you are not.

Practice empathy

See if you can figure out where they are coming from. This can help you to be more empathetic towards their feelings and needs.

Be supportive

Be there for your siblings when they need you. Offer your support and encouragement when they are going through a tough time.

Show appreciation

Show your siblings that you appreciate them. Say thank you to them each time they do something nice for you and let them know that you love them.

Your grandparents

I wanted to talk about how to improve your relationship with your grandparents. Our grandparents are some of the wisest and most experienced people in our lives and they love us and are so proud of us. Sometimes it can be difficult to connect with them - maybe they live far away, or maybe you just feel like you don't have a lot in common with them. But building a strong relationship with your grandparents can be so rewarding, and it's definitely worth the effort.

That's why I've put together 10 tips on how to get along better with your grandparents. Whether you see them all the time or just on holidays, these tips can help you strengthen your bond and make some amazing memories with your grandparents. So, let's dive in!

Ask them about their life

Grandparents have lived a long time and have lots of stories to share. Ask them about their childhood, how they met your grandparent, or any other interesting anecdotes.

Listen to their advice

They've been around the block a few times, and their experience can be really valuable. Listen to their advice and take it to heart.

Show an interest in their hobbies

Whether it's gardening, knitting, or woodworking, show an interest in their hobbies and ask them to teach you.

Share your interests with them

Introduce your grandparents to your hobbies and interests. They might be interested in learning something new!

Spend quality time together

Whether it's watching a movie or playing a board game, spend quality time with your grandparents and make some memories together.

Offer to help with chores

If your grandparents need help with household chores, offer to lend a hand. It shows that you care and appreciate them.

Respect their opinions

You might not always agree with your grandparents' opinions, but it's important to respect them nonetheless.

Celebrate special occasions

Make an effort to celebrate special occasions like birthdays or holidays with your grandparents. It shows that you care and want to spend time with them.

Send them letters or cards

A simple gesture like sending a letter or card can really brighten your grandparents' day and let them know you're thinking of them.

Show gratitude

Remember to say thank you for all that your grandparents do for you. A little bit of gratitude can go a long way in strengthening your relationship with them.

Your aunts & uncles

Family is an important part of our lives, and our aunts and uncles can be some of our most influential family members. They can offer advice, support, and a different perspective on life. Here are some nice ways to grow your relationships with your aunts & uncles.

Keep in touch, even if you don't see them often, make an effort to keep in touch with your aunts and uncles through text, phone calls, or social media. Show an interest in their life. Ask them about their job, hobbies, or any exciting news they have to share.

Attend family gatherings. Family gatherings like reunions or holidays are a great opportunity to spend time with your aunts and uncles.

Help with party planning. If your family is hosting a party or get-together, offer to help your aunts and uncles with the planning and preparation.

Share your own interests. Introduce your aunts and uncles to your hobbies and interests. They might have similar interests or be interested in learning something new! Listen to their advice. Your aunts and uncles have life experience and advice that can be really valuable. Listen to what they have to say and take it to heart.

Respect their boundaries. If your aunts and uncles need space or have boundaries, respect them and don't push them.

Celebrate special occasions. Make an effort to celebrate special occasions like birthdays or anniversaries with your aunts and uncles. It shows that you care and want to spend time with them. Send them little gifts or cards - a small gesture like sending a thoughtful card or gift can really brighten their day and let them know you're thinking of them.

Show gratitude. Don't forget to say thank you for all that your aunts and uncles do for you. People really appreciate this and it can really help to strengthen your relationship with them.

How to get along better with your family

Ask for help

As a teenager, it can sometimes feel like we need to handle everything on our own. We want to prove that we're independent and can handle anything that comes our way. However, the truth is that no one can do it all alone, and sometimes we need to ask for help. And who better to turn to for help than our family?

Firstly, our family members know us better than anyone else. They know our strengths, weaknesses, and the things that make us tick. This means they can offer more personalized advice and guidance when we need it.

Secondly, our family members have likely gone through similar experiences in their own lives, so they can offer valuable insights and perspectives. They may have dealt with similar challenges or made similar mistakes, and can share what they learned from those experiences.

Finally, our family members are often the most reliable and trustworthy people in our lives. We can count on them to be there for us when we need support or encouragement. They can be a source of comfort and strength during difficult times.

In short, asking our family for help is important because they know us best, have valuable experiences to share, and can be a reliable source of support. Let your family when you need help – they're there to help you!

Saying sorry

As a teenager, admitting when we're wrong or when we've made a mistake can be a difficult thing to do. Saying sorry can make us feel vulnerable or embarrassed. However, it's important to remember that apologizing is an essential part of building healthy relationships with others.

When we make a mistake or hurt someone's feelings, saying sorry shows that we recognize our error and that we care about how our actions affected others. This helps to build trust and respect in our relationships.

Additionally, when we apologize, we create an opportunity for forgiveness and healing. We're able to acknowledge the hurt we caused and take steps to make amends, which can help to repair damaged relationships.

Learning when to say sorry also helps us to take responsibility for our actions and to develop a sense of accountability. It can be tempting to shift the blame onto others or to make excuses for our behavior, but ultimately this can erode trust and respect in our relationships. Taking ownership of our mistakes and apologizing when necessary shows that we're mature and responsible.

In short, knowing when to say sorry is important because it helps to build healthy relationships, encourages forgiveness and healing, and helps us to develop a sense of accountability. If you make a mistake or hurt someone's feelings, take a deep breath, be brave, and say sorry. It'll make a big difference!

Never go to bed on an argument

As a teenager, it's natural to have disagreements or arguments with family members, friends, or even romantic partners. While it's important to express our thoughts and feelings, it's equally important to know when to put the argument to rest.

One important rule to follow is to never go to bed on an argument. This means that we should try to resolve the conflict before the end of the day, instead of letting it fester overnight. There are several reasons why this is important. Firstly, going to bed on an argument can make us feel anxious. It can also make it harder to get a good night's rest, which can affect our mood and productivity the next day.

Secondly, unresolved conflicts can lead to resentment and bitterness over time, which can damage our relationships. When we hold onto grudges or negative feelings towards someone, it can create a toxic dynamic that's difficult to repair.

Finally, resolving conflicts quickly allows us to move forward and focus on the positive aspects of our relationships. We can let go of negative emotions and work towards a more positive, loving connection with the people in our lives.

So, the next time you find yourself in an argument with someone, try to resolve the conflict before the end of the day. It'll make a big difference in your life and your relationships!

See life from someone else's perspective

As a teenager, it's easy to get caught up in our own thoughts, feelings, and experiences. We're going through a lot of changes and challenges as we grow up, which can make it hard to see things from other people's perspectives. However, it's incredibly important to try to do so.

One way to broaden our perspective is to make an effort to see life from someone else's point of view. This means putting ourselves in someone else's shoes and trying to understand their thoughts, feelings, and experiences. It requires empathy and an open mind, which can be difficult at times, but it's a skill that's worth cultivating.

There are several reasons why this is important. Firstly, it helps us to be more compassionate and understanding towards others. When we take the time to see life from someone else's perspective, we can gain a deeper appreciation for what they're going through and respond with greater kindness and empathy.

Secondly, it can help us to resolve conflicts more effectively. When we're able to see things from someone else's perspective, we can find common ground and work towards a solution that benefits everyone involved.

Finally, seeing life from someone else's perspective can broaden our own worldview and help us to grow as individuals. It allows us to challenge our assumptions and biases, and can lead to greater understanding and tolerance of people who are different from us.

If you can't say anything nice, don't say anything at all

The saying "If you can't say anything nice, don't say anything at all" is a valuable lesson for teenagers to learn. As we grow up, we may encounter situations where we feel frustrated, angry, or hurt by others. It's important to remember that how we choose to respond can have a big impact on our relationships and on our own well-being.

When we speak negatively or hurtfully to others, it can damage our relationships and cause others to feel upset or offended. This can create tension and conflict, which can be difficult to repair. Also, when we speak negatively or hurtfully, it can also impact our own mental health and well-being. It can create feelings of guilt, shame, or regret in ourselves, which can be hard to deal with.

On the other hand, when we choose to speak kindly and respectfully, it can strengthen our relationships and create positive feelings between ourselves and others. It can create an atmosphere of trust and mutual respect, which can help to maintain healthy relationships.

Learning to control our words and emotions is an important part of growing up. By taking a moment to reflect on how we're feeling before we speak, we can make sure that we're not saying anything hurtful or negative. It's okay to express our feelings, but try and do this so it comes across as respectful and constructive.

Offer to help out

Offering to help out a family member is really important because it shows that we care about their well-being and are willing to contribute to the family unit. As teenagers, it's easy to get caught up in our own lives and responsibilities, but it's important to remember that our family members may also need our support and assistance.

When we offer to help out a family member, it can have a positive impact on both them and us. For the family member, it can alleviate some stress or workload, and help them feel supported and appreciated. For us, it can give us a sense of purpose and fulfillment, and can also help us develop important life skills such as responsibility and empathy.

It's important to be specific when offering to help out a family member. Instead of just saying, "Let me know if you need anything," we should think about what specific tasks or responsibilities we can take on. For example, we can offer to do the grocery shopping, help with household chores, or assist with caring for younger siblings or grandparents.

Offering to help out a family member can also help to build trust and strengthen our relationships. When we show that we are willing to contribute to the family unit, our family members are more likely to trust and rely on us. This can help to create a more harmonious and supportive family environment.

Give a compliment

Sharing a compliment with a family member is a simple yet powerful way to strengthen our relationships with them. As teenagers, it's easy to get caught up in our own lives and forget to show appreciation for those around us. However, taking the time to share a kind word or gesture can make a huge difference in how we connect with our family members.

Sharing a compliment with a family member can also have a positive impact on our own well-being. By focusing on the positive qualities of those around us, we can shift our own mindset to one of gratitude and positivity. This can help us to feel more connected to our family members and improve our overall mood.

We should take the time to think about what we appreciate about them and be specific in our praise. For example, instead of just saying "You're great," we can say something like, "I really appreciate how supportive you are of me and always make time to listen to my problems."

Finally, sharing a compliment with a family member can help to build trust and strengthen our relationships. When we show appreciation for others, they're more likely to feel valued and respected. This can create a positive feedback loop, where we feel more connected to our family members and they in turn feel more connected to us.

School

Why school?

As a teenager, it's totally normal to have days where you're just not feeling school. But even on those days, it's important to remember that school is really important for your future.

Here's why: first of all, school is where you learn a lot of the skills and knowledge you'll need to succeed in life. Whether you're learning math, science, history, or English, you're gaining a lot of valuable information that will help you later on. Plus, when you're in school, you're being taught by experts who know a ton about their subjects, so you're getting a really high-quality education.

But it's not just about the facts and figures. School is also where you develop a lot of important life skills that you can use throughout your life. You're learning how to manage your time effectively, how to be responsible and get things done, and how to work well with others. These are all skills that employers really value, so they'll be really helpful when you start looking for jobs in the future.

Another important aspect of school is that it's a great place to make friends and build relationships with your peers. When you're in class and working on group projects, you're interacting with a lot of different people from all walks of life. This is a really valuable experience, because it helps you to learn how to be more empathetic, understanding, and tolerant of others.

School can be a great way to explore your interests and figure out what you want to do in the future. Whether you're interested in science, art, music, or something else entirely, there are a lot of resources available to you in school. You can take classes, join clubs or extracurricular activities, and even talk to your teachers and counselors to get advice and guidance.

School can also open up a world of opportunities for you in terms of your future careers and education. By performing well academically, you may be eligible for scholarships or acceptance into prestigious universities. You may also have the opportunity to explore different career paths through internships, job shadowing, and other training opportunities.

How to be successful in school

Attend all your classes

Going to every class is the foundation of being successful in school. Even if you don't feel like it, try to show up every day.

Take good notes

Taking effective notes in class will help you remember the material better and make studying for exams easier.

Stay organized

Keep track of assignments and deadlines in a planner or calendar to avoid missing important due dates.

Participate in class

Engage in class discussions and ask questions when you don't understand something. This shows your teacher that you are interested and invested in your education.

Manage your time wisely

Balance your schoolwork with extracurricular activities, family time, and friends. Avoid procrastination and try to study a little bit each day.

Find a study group

Collaborating with peers is a great way to share ideas and learn from one another.

Seek help when needed

Always ask for help from your teachers, peers, or tutors. They are there to support you.

Take breaks

You will need to take breaks and recharge your brain. Take a walk or listen to music to clear your mind.

Stay focused

Avoid distractions during study time, such as social media or TV. Put your phone away or turn it off if necessary.

Believe in yourself

Have confidence in your abilities and don't be too hard on yourself if you don't get something right away. Believe that you can do it, and you will!

Posture & health

Good posture is important for both physical and mental health, especially during long hours spent sitting in school or studying.

Having good posture as a teenager is important for long-term health because it can prevent problems later in life. Poor posture can cause a range of issues, including a sore back and neck, headaches, and even breathing problems. Over time, these problems can become chronic and affect your overall well-being.

Additionally, having good posture can improve your balance and coordination, which can reduce your risk of falls and other injuries. Good posture can also help you stay at a healthy weight, as it encourages you to use your core muscles and stay active.

But good posture isn't just about physical health - it can also impact your mental health. When you sit up straight and have good posture, you can feel more confident and self-assured. This can help you feel happier and reduce stress and anxiety.

So, by practicing good posture as a teenager, you're not only helping your current health, but you're also investing in your future well-being. Here are some tips you can try:

Start to notice your picture

Become aware of when you are slouching or leaning forward. Once we become aware of our habits, we are in a great position to improve them.

Adjust your chair and desk

Make sure your chair and desk are at the right height. Put your feet flat on the ground. Have your knees at a 90-degree angle.

Take breaks

Remember to take little breaks during the day to stretch and move around. Sitting for too long can be harmful to your health.

Use a cushion

If your chair is uncomfortable, use a cushion to support your back.

Exercise

Regular exercise can help strengthen your core and back muscles, which will make it easier to maintain good posture.

How heavy is your school bag?

As a teenager, carrying heavy school bags can really stress and hurt your body, and potentially lead to a range of health issues. When you carry a heavy backpack, it can cause poor posture, as you may need to lean forward to balance the weight on your back. You can end up with back pain, neck pain, and headaches. If your bag is really heavy it can also lead to muscle strains and injuries, especially if you're not lifting it properly. Over time, these injuries can become chronic and affect your daily life. It's important to try and minimize the weight of your school bag and only carry what you need for the day. Consider using a backpack with wide, padded straps and a waist belt to distribute the weight evenly. And if you must carry a heavy load, be sure to lift your backpack properly by bending your knees and using your leg muscles, rather than your back.

Remember, good posture not only helps you physically, but it can boost your confidence levels and make you feel more alert and engaged in class and help you to feel better when you are studying.

Learning & Hard Work Vs. Talent.

Being successful in life doesn't always depend on your innate talent. Quite often the smartest kids in school are not the most successful as adults. Memorizing facts for tests is a huge part of school, but not everyone finds this easy. So if you are not the highest-achieving student in your class, this does not mean that you will struggle in adult life.

What truly matters is your determination, ambition, and hard work towards your chosen career path. If you are focused, ambitious and work hard at what you choose to do, you could be a millionaire! And this could be in anything from being a scientist, a programmer, an author, a sportsperson, TV personality, creating your own range of artwork, running an online business from your laptop while traveling the world, or becoming a successful cafe or restaurant owner.

The possibilities are endless as long as you stay focused and work towards your goals. You can do anything you decide to do, if you work hard enough.

Success in school & life

Very often the people who are very successful in both business and their jobs as adults have a positive mindset. And you can start practicing this in school! Be early or on time. Smile & say hello & be friendly. Offer to help out. Be kind to someone who needs help. Always do a little more than was asked for. When you admire something someone has done, tell them and give them a compliment.

You might not know, but having a positive mindset can be a big factor in being successful in life. It's true! And the best part about it is that you can start practicing this mindset in school.

Showing up early or on time, smiling and greeting people, being friendly and offering to help out are all great ways to start. Also, try being kind to someone who needs help and always doing a little more than what was asked for. Give someone an unexpected compliment.

These small strategies can really help to make you a likable and successful person. Being on-time, hard-working, kind, positive and nice to be around are huge factors that will help you to be super successful - no matter what path you follow in life - and it works for home, school, college, jobs and when you're running your own business.

Homework

Homework is an essential part of school life. However, it's not always easy to stay motivated and focused when there are so many distractions around us. But don't panic, as there are several tips and tricks that can make your homework easier to complete. In this guide, we'll share some practical advice on how to approach your homework more efficiently, so you have more time to enjoy your hobbies and downtime. Whether you're struggling with procrastination, time management, or finding the right environment to study in, we've got you covered. So let's discover how you can make your homework a more manageable task.

Create a schedule

Set a specific time for homework each day and stick to it. This way, you won't procrastinate or forget about it.

Find a quiet and comfortable workspace

Choose a spot where you can focus without distractions, such as the TV or noisy siblings.

Get organized

Keep all your homework materials in one place and get everything together that you'll need before you start.

Break down the assignment

If you have a big project or a lot of homework, break it down into smaller, more manageable tasks. This will help you avoid feeling overwhelmed.

Take breaks

It's important to take regular breaks to rest your mind and avoid burnout. Take a short walk or do some stretches to refresh yourself.

Avoid multitasking

Do one thing at a time instead of trying to do multiple things at once. This will help you concentrate and be more efficient.

Ask for help

Don't be afraid to ask your teacher, a parent or a tutor for help if you need it. They are there to support you.

Reward yourself

Once you complete your homework, give yourself a reward, such as watching your favorite show or having a snack. This will motivate you to finish your work more quickly next time.

Fixing situations in school

School can be tough and as a teenager it's normal to encounter some difficult situations. Maybe you're struggling with a particular class, dealing with a mean girl or a bully, or feeling overwhelmed by the pressure to fit in. Whatever has happened, it's important to have strategies in place to help you navigate these situations and come out on top. In this guide, we'll explore 8 tips on what you can do when facing a challenging situation in school, so you can handle it and feel confident in yourself.

Take a deep breath: When faced with a difficult situation, the first thing to do is to take a deep breath and take a step back. This will help you think more clearly and rationally about the situation.

Seek help: Don't be afraid to seek help from a teacher, counselor or parent. They can provide valuable support and advice to help you navigate the situation.

Communicate: Try to communicate effectively with the other party involved. This means listening to their perspective and expressing your own thoughts and feelings in a respectful and constructive manner.

Take responsibility: If you are at fault, take responsibility for your actions and say sorry if you need to. This can go a long way in resolving the situation and rebuilding relationships.

Look for a solution: Instead of dwelling on the problem, focus on finding a solution that works for everyone involved. Brainstorm ideas and be open to compromise.

Stay positive: It's easy to get down on yourself and the situation, but try to stay positive and optimistic. Believe that you can find a solution and things will work out in the end.

Take a break: If the situation is causing you a lot of stress, take a break from it. Go for a walk, listen to music or try something you love to take your mind off it.

Learn from it: Every difficult situation is an opportunity to learn and grow. Reflect on what happened, what you could have done differently and how you can use this experience to improve yourself and your relationships in the future.

Dealing with peer pressure & bullies

As a teenager, you may face situations at school or when socializing with friends, where you feel pressured to do things you're not comfortable with or may even encounter bullies who make you feel helpless. These situations can be tough to deal with, but you must remember that you're not alone and that there are ways to handle them. Here are some ways on how to deal with peer pressure and bullies so that you can feel more confident and in control in these challenging situations. Remember, your safety and well-being should always come first, and there's no shame in seeking help when you need it.

Surround yourself with positive people

Make sure the people in your life uplift you and help you to grow into the best version of yourself. Seek out friends who share similar values and interests.

Trust your instincts

If something doesn't feel right, trust your gut. Don't do something just because your peers are doing it.

Learn to say "no"

Saying "no" is really tricky, but it's important to stand up for yourself and what you believe in. Practice saying "no" with confidence – like you really mean it.

Talk to someone you trust

Whether it's a parent, teacher, or counselor, talking to someone you trust can help you navigate difficult situations and make better decisions.

Avoid dangerous situations

If you are in a situation that feels unsafe or uncomfortable, remove yourself from it as quickly as possible.

Use humor

Sometimes using humor can diffuse a tense situation and help you stand up for yourself without being confrontational.

Practice self-care

Taking care of your body and emotions can help you feel more confident and better equipped to handle difficult situations.

Don't retaliate

If someone is bullying you, it's important to not retaliate with violence or aggression. Instead, try to remain calm and seek help from a trusted adult.

Remember that it's not your fault

No one deserves to be bullied or pressured into doing something they don't want to do. Remember that it's not your fault and seek support from those around you.

Making friends

How to make friends

Making friends as a teenager can be tough, especially if you're starting at a new school or trying to break out of your comfort zone. But don't worry, there are plenty of things you can do to make new connections and build lasting friendships. I will share 11 tips on how to make friends as a teenager. These tips range from joining a club or group to using social media to connect with others. So, let's get started and find out how you can make new friends.

Be yourself

Always remember to be yourself. Don't try to be someone you're not just to fit in.

Smile and be friendly

A friendly smile can really help to make someone feel welcomed and comfortable around you. Be friendly and approachable.

Join a club or group

Joining a club or group can be a great way to make friends who love the same things you do.

Volunteer

Volunteering your time for free is a nice way to meet new people and give back to your community at the same time.

Attend school events

Whether it's a school dance or a football game, attending school events is a great way to meet new people.

Start a conversation

Don't be shy! Start talking to someone you don't know. Ask about their interests or hobbies.

Be a good listener

When someone is talking to you, listen attentively so they know you are interested in what they have to say.

Show interest in others

Ask questions and show a genuine interest in others. People love to talk about themselves.

Treat people like you'd like to be treated yourself.

Kindness is one of our super strengths!

Don't be afraid to be vulnerable

Opening up to others can help build trust and deepen friendships.

Be patient

Building friendships takes time, so be patient and don't give up if it doesn't happen overnight.

Being a good friend

Being a teenager can be challenging, and having good friends to support you can make all the difference. But, it's not just about having friends, it's also about being a good friend yourself. So, whether you're looking to strengthen your current friendships or build new ones, these tips will help you become the best friend you can be. Let's dive in!

Be trustworthy: One of the most important things in any friendship is trust. Be honest and keep your promises.

Be a good listener: When your friend is talking to you, really listen to what they're saying. Show that you care and that you're there for them.

Be supportive: Your friends may go through tough times, and it's important to be there for them. Offer support and encouragement when they need it.

Be respectful: Respect your friends' boundaries and opinions, even if they differ from your own. Show that you value their thoughts and feelings.

Be inclusive: Include your friends in your plans and activities. Don't leave anyone out or make anyone feel excluded.

Be reliable: Be someone your friends can count on. If you say you'll do something, follow through on it.

Be fun: Laughter is often the best medicine, so be someone who brings joy and fun into your friends' lives.

Be forgiving: Everyone makes mistakes, and it's important to be forgiving and understanding when your friends mess up.

Communicate openly: Be open and honest with your friends. If something is bothering you, talk about it calmly and respectfully.

Don't live in the past. It's better to look forwards and to stay as positive as we can be.

Don't burn your bridges.

A little kindness goes a long way. Being kind can change the world for the people you know.

Make time for your friends. Check in with them, see how they are and offer to help them whenever you can.

Remember, being a good friend takes effort and practice, but the rewards of strong, supportive friendships are worth it. So, put these tips into action and be the best friend you can be!

Setting boundaries & saying no

As a teenager, it can be easy to feel like you need to say yes to everything in order to fit in or be liked by others. However, it's important for teenagers to be able to set boundaries and say no. Here's why:

Protecting your physical and mental health

Saying yes to everything isn't the best idea as it can cause you stress. By setting boundaries and saying no, you can protect their physical and mental health.

Developing healthy relationships

Being able to set boundaries and say no is a sign of self-respect and shows that you value your own needs and feelings. This can lead to healthier relationships based on mutual respect.

Building self-esteem and confidence

Saying no can be difficult, but it's important for teenagers to develop the confidence and self-esteem to stand up for themselves when necessary.

Avoiding risky situations

Sometimes saying no can be a way to avoid risky or dangerous situations. It's important for teenagers to be able to say no if they feel uncomfortable or unsafe.

Learning important life skills

Setting boundaries and saying no are important life skills that teenagers will use throughout their lives, whether in school, work, or personal relationships.

Setting boundaries and saying no are important skills for you to develop. It can help you protect their physical and mental health, build healthy relationships, develop self-esteem and confidence, avoid risky situations, and learn important life skills.

When it's OK to stop a friendship

As a teenager, friendships can be an important part of your life, but sometimes it may become necessary to say goodbye to a friendship. Here are some situations when it may be okay to say goodbye to a friendship:

Lack of trust: Trust is a key component of any healthy friendship. If you find that you can't trust your friend or they constantly break your trust, it may be time to say goodbye.

Negative influence: If a friend is constantly engaging in behavior that is harmful or negative, it may be best to distance yourself from that friendship.

Different values: As you grow and mature, your values may change. If you find that your values and beliefs are no longer in line with your friend's, it may be time to move on.

Is it unfixable? If there are issues in the friendship that you've tried to work through but can't seem to resolve, it may be time to say goodbye.

Toxicity: If a friendship is consistently negative, draining, or even abusive, it's important to prioritize your own well-being and say goodbye.

It's important to remember that saying goodbye to a friendship can be a difficult decision, but sometimes it's necessary for your own personal growth and well-being. You can end friendships that are no longer serving you, and to focus on building relationships with people who support and uplift you.

Home

Helping your family and doing chores around the house as a teenager is important for several reasons.

Contributing to the household

When everyone in the family pitches in with chores, it makes the workload more manageable for everyone. By doing your part, you're contributing to a positive family dynamic and helping to create a clean and comfortable living space for everyone.

Showing appreciation

By doing chores, you're showing your family that you appreciate the work they do to keep the household running smoothly. This can create a sense of gratitude and respect within the family and help to strengthen your relationships with each other.

Improving your mental health.

Keeping your living space clean and organized makes you feel better. Studies have shown that living in a messy environment can give you anxiety, while a clean and organized space can promote a sense of calm and well-being.

Setting a good example.

By taking initiative and doing your chores without being asked, you're setting a good example for your siblings and other family members. This can help create a positive family culture where everyone takes responsibility for their actions and contributes to the household.

Making chores at home fun

Making home chores fun might seem unlikely, but there are definitely ways to make it less boring and maybe even enjoyable.

Turn up the music

Turn on your favorite music and turn up the volume. This can help you get into a rhythm and make the chore go by faster. You can even create a playlist specifically for doing chores.

Gamify it

Turn chores into a game by setting goals and giving yourself rewards for completing them. For example, you could set a timer and try to finish a task before the timer runs out, or you could challenge yourself - how many dishes you can wash in a certain amount of time? Can you get all your chores done in 20 minutes? Set a timer and find out!

Get a chore buddy

Doing chores with a friend or family member can make them feel less tedious. You can chat, joke around, or even race each other to see who finishes their tasks first.

Make it a workout

Some chores, like vacuuming or scrubbing the bathtub, can actually be pretty good exercise. Try to approach these tasks with a "let's get a workout in" mentality, and see if you can break a sweat while you're cleaning.

Add some creativity

You can make chores more interesting by adding a creative twist to them. For example, if you're dusting, challenge yourself to arrange the objects in a fun or unique way. Or if you're folding laundry, see if you can come up with a new folding technique.

A life without nagging

It can be tough if you feel that your parents are nagging you about home chores, but there are a few ways you can try to improve the situation.

Firstly, it's important to understand that your parents are likely just trying to teach you responsibility and help you develop good habits for when you're older. However, constant nagging can be frustrating, so here are a few tips that might help:

Take the initiative

Try to do your chores before your parents ask you to. This will show them that you are responsible and don't need constant reminders. If you have a regular chore schedule, make sure you stick to it consistently.

Communicate

Talk to your parents. Tell them that you understand the importance of doing chores, but that constant nagging is making you feel frustrated. Ask them if there are any specific things they would like you to improve on and work on those things proactively.

Negotiate

If you feel like you're being overwhelmed with too many chores, try negotiating with your parents. Offer to do some extra chores one day if they'll let you off the hook for another day. Try to find a compromise that works for both of you.

Be respectful

Remember that your parents are doing their best to help you grow into a responsible adult. Even if you don't agree with their methods, try to be respectful and understand that they're coming from a place of love.

In summary, taking the initiative, communicating, negotiating, and being respectful can all help to reduce the nagging from your parents about home chores.

Bedroom cleaning tips

We've all got busy lives, and as a teenager it's easy to get caught up in schoolwork, hobbies, and socializing. But it's important to keep your bedroom clean and organized. Not only does a tidy room look better, but it can also help you feel more relaxed and focused. It will involve a little work on your part, but these chores are quick and easy to do, and they can make a big difference in the overall appearance and feel of your room. Here are some ideas to keep your bedroom clean and organized:

Make your bed

Making your bed every morning is a quick and easy way to start the day off on the right foot. It also makes your room look instantly tidier and more put-together.

Dust surfaces

Dust can quickly accumulate on surfaces like shelves, desks, and dressers. Taking a few minutes to dust these surfaces regularly can help keep your room looking clean and fresh.

Vacuuming or sweeping

Depending on the type of flooring in your room, you may need to vacuum or sweep regularly to keep it clean. This is especially important if you have carpet, as dust and dirt can quickly get trapped in the fibers.

Laundry

Keeping your dirty laundry off the floor and in a hamper can help keep your room smelling fresh and looking tidy. You can also take responsibility for washing and folding your own laundry if you're able to.

Decluttering

Going through your belongings regularly and throwing out anything you no longer need, can help keep your room organized and clutter-free.

Wiping down surfaces

It's a good idea to wipe down surfaces like countertops, mirrors, and windows on a regular basis to keep them clean and free of smudges or fingerprints.

Organizing your closet

Keeping your clothes and accessories organized in your closet can help make it easier to find what you're looking for and keep your room looking tidy.

8 house cleaning hacks

Here are 8 house cleaning hacks to make cleaning a little easier and more efficient.

Use a timer: Setting a timer for 10-15 minutes can help you stay focused and motivated while cleaning. It also helps you break up the cleaning into smaller tasks so it doesn't feel overwhelming.

Create a cleaning playlist: Listening to music can make cleaning more fun and enjoyable. Create a playlist of your favorite upbeat songs to listen to while cleaning.

Use vinegar and baking soda for tough stains: If you have a tough stain on a surface, try mixing equal parts vinegar and baking soda into a paste. Apply the paste to the stain then wait a few minutes before wiping it away with a cloth. This can work wonders on everything from carpet stains to bathtub grime.

Clean your microwave with lemon: If your microwave is looking a little worse for wear, try cutting a lemon in half and microwaving it for a few minutes. The steam from the lemon can help loosen any grime or stuck-on food, making it easier to wipe away with a cloth.

Clean your showerhead with vinegar: If your shower head is clogged with mineral deposits, try filling a plastic bag with vinegar and attaching it to the showerhead with a rubber band. Let it sit for a few hours before removing the bag and running the shower to rinse away any remaining vinegar and mineral deposits.

Use a lint roller on lampshades: Lampshades can quickly accumulate dust and pet hair, making them look dingy. Try using a lint roller to quickly and easily remove any debris from the surface of the shade.

Clean blinds with a sock: Instead of struggling to clean your blinds with a traditional duster or cloth, try using a clean sock. Slip the sock onto your hand and run your hand along each individual slat to remove any dust or debris.

Use a toothbrush for hard-to-reach areas: If you have a hard-to-reach area that's looking a little grungy, try using a toothbrush to scrub away any dirt or grime. This works especially well on areas like grout, which can be difficult to clean with a traditional cloth.

How to change a lightbulb

Changing a lightbulb might seem like a small task, but it's one that can come in handy at any time. Here are the steps to follow:

Turn off the power: Before you begin, make sure the light switch is turned off and the power to the light fixture is off. This will prevent you from getting shocked while changing the bulb.

Allow the bulb to cool: If the light fixture was recently turned on, wait a few minutes for the bulb to cool down before attempting to remove it. Hot bulbs can be fragile and easily break when handled.

Remove the old bulb: If the bulb is a screw-in type, gently twist it counterclockwise to loosen it from the socket. If the bulb is a push-in type, gently push the bulb in and twist it counterclockwise until it comes free from the socket.

Check the wattage: Before installing the new bulb, check the wattage of the old bulb to make sure you're replacing it with the correct wattage. Using a bulb with too high of a wattage can be a fire hazard.

Install the new bulb: Gently insert the new bulb into the socket, and twist it clockwise until it is snugly in place.

Turn the power back on: When the new bulb is in, turn the power back on and test the light to make sure it is working properly.

And there you have it! Changing a lightbulb is a simple task that can be done quickly and easily with a little bit of caution and know-how.

Smoke alarms

A smoke alarm is an essential safety feature that can save your life in the event of a fire. It is designed to detect smoke and alert you to the danger, giving you time to evacuate the building and call for help. Smoke alarms are especially important at night when you are asleep and may not be able to smell the smoke from a fire.

To check your smoke alarm, follow these simple steps:

Press the test button: Most smoke alarms have a test button that you can press to check if the alarm is working properly. Press and hold the button until you hear the alarm sound.

Listen for the alarm sound: If you hear the alarm sound, then the alarm is working properly. If the alarm does not sound, try replacing the battery and testing it again. If it still doesn't work, you may need to replace the entire smoke alarm.

Test the batteries: If your smoke alarm uses batteries, it's important to test them regularly and replace them as needed. Some alarms will beep to let you know when the batteries are running low, but it's a good idea to check them manually every six months or so.

Remember, smoke alarms are an important safety feature that can help protect you and your family in the event of a fire. By checking your smoke alarm regularly and replacing the batteries as needed, you can ensure that it is working properly and providing you with the protection you need. Knowing how to check a smoke alarm could save your life one day.

Hobbies

A hobby can change your life. I'm being serious! What starts off as a hobby can end up as a professional career that you love.

Photography

Many people enjoy taking photos as a hobby, but some go on to pursue it as a career. Professional photographers can work in a variety of fields, such as wedding photography, fashion photography, or photojournalism.

Writing

Writing can be a hobby that turns into a successful career for many people. Whether it's writing novels, non-fiction books, or screenplays, those who have a passion for writing can often turn it into a career as a writer or author.

Cooking

Some people who love cooking as a hobby turn it into a career as a chef or restaurateur. They may attend culinary school or work their way up in the food industry, eventually opening their own restaurant.

Fitness

Many people who are passionate about fitness turn it into a career as a personal trainer or fitness instructor. They may start by teaching classes at a gym or working with clients one-on-one, eventually building their own successful fitness business.

Music

Some people who enjoy playing music as a hobby go on to pursue it as a career. They may become professional musicians, music teachers, or work in the music industry in other ways, such as music production or audio engineering.

These are some ideas of hobbies that can turn into successful careers. The key is to find something that you're passionate about and pursue it with dedication and hard work. Who knows, your hobby may just turn into your dream job!

You can also turn your teenage hobby into a great part-time job, or a job overseas. Love skiing? Get a winter job as a skiing instructor when you're older. Love horse riding? Get a part-time job teaching at a local riding school while you're in college.

Hobbies can help you become more creative express yourself in new and exciting ways. Whether it's painting, writing, or playing music, having a hobby can help you explore your creative potential and unleash your imagination.

A hobby can provide a sense of accomplishment and build your confidence hugely. Hobbies can give you a sense of purpose and achievement. When you set goals for yourself and work towards them, you can experience a great sense of satisfaction and pride when you achieve them.

Hobbies can be a great way to unwind and de-stress after a long day. They can help you relax, clear your mind, and forget about your worries for a little while. Hobbies can also help you build new skills and improve existing ones. Whether it's learning a new language, mastering a musical instrument, or developing your cooking skills, hobbies can help you develop your talents and abilities.

Many hobbies involve connecting with others who share similar interests. Joining a club or group related to your hobby can help you meet new people and make new friends.

When you excel at a hobby or achieve a goal you've set for yourself, it can boost your self-confidence and self-esteem. This can translate into other areas of your life, such as school or work. Hobbies can also be a healthy way to channel your energy and emotions. Instead of turning to negative outlets, such as drugs or alcohol, hobbies can provide a positive and fulfilling way to spend your time.

Find a hobby you enjoy

Let's see how you can find a hobby you'll enjoy.

Try new things: Be open to trying new activities that you haven't done before. Whether it's a new sport, art form, or musical instrument, exploring new things can help you find what you're passionate about.

Look for inspiration: Look to your role models or people you admire for inspiration. What hobbies do they enjoy? What do they do outside of work or school? You might find something you're interested in by following their lead.

Explore your interests: Think about the things you enjoy doing or learning about. For example, if you love reading, you might enjoy writing or joining a book club. If you enjoy being outdoors, you might enjoy hiking or gardening.

Consider your personality: Think about what type of activities align with your personality. If you're introverted, you might enjoy hobbies like reading or playing video games. If you're extroverted, you might enjoy team sports or performing.

Join a club or group: Joining a club or group related to your interests can help you meet new people and discover new hobbies. You might find a new passion by connecting with others who share similar interests.

Look online: There are plenty of online resources that can help you find new hobbies. Websites like Meetup.com, for example, can connect you with local groups and events related to your interests.

Experiment: Don't be afraid to try out different hobbies and activities until you find something you enjoy. It may take some time to find the right fit, but the journey can be just as rewarding as the destination.

Remember, hobbies are a great way to explore your interests and passions, meet new people, and build skills. Finding a hobby you enjoy can be a lifelong pursuit, so don't be afraid to keep trying new things until you find the one that's right for you!

Food, cooking & healthy eating habits

As a teenager, you might have heard the phrase "you are what you eat". It's true! What you eat can affect your health, your energy levels, and even your mood. That's why everyone needs to learn how to cook and eat healthy food. Don't worry, it's quite easy! In fact, cooking can be a lot of fun and you can get really creative too. Plus, when you cook your own meals, you get to choose the ingredients and you can make sure they're healthy and delicious. So, let's dive in and learn about cooking and healthy eating.

Grocery shopping

As a teenager, you might be starting to take more responsibility for your own meals and grocery shopping. It can be overwhelming to navigate the aisles of the grocery store and make healthy choices, especially if you're on a budget. That's why I've put together 9 tips to help you make the most out of your grocery shopping trips. By following these tips, you can save money, make healthy choices, and even enjoy the process of shopping for food.

Plan your meals ahead: Before heading to the grocery store, take some time to plan out your meals for the week. This will help you know exactly what ingredients you need to buy, and it will also prevent you from buying unnecessary items.

Make a list: Once you've planned your meals, make a grocery list. This will help you stay organized and focused while you're at the store.

Stick to the perimeter: Generally, the healthiest foods are located around the perimeter of the grocery store. This includes fresh produce, dairy, and meat. Try to stick to these areas as much as possible.

Read labels: When you're buying packaged foods, make sure to read the labels. Look for foods that are low in sugar, sodium, and saturated fat.

Buy in bulk: Buying in bulk can be a great way to save money, especially if you're buying staples like rice or beans.

Choose fresh produce: Whenever possible, choose fresh produce over canned or frozen. Fresh fruits and vegetables are often more nutritious and flavorful.

Avoid processed foods: Processed foods, like chips and soda, are often high in calories, sugar, and sodium. Try to avoid them as much as possible.

Don't shop when you're hungry: Shopping when you're hungry can lead to impulse buys and unhealthy choices. Make sure to eat a snack or meal before heading to the store.

Stick to your budget: Set a budget for your grocery shopping and try to stick to it. This will help you avoid overspending and make sure you have enough money for other things you need.

Fridge hacks

Keeping your fridge organized and clean is an important part of maintaining a healthy and efficient kitchen. A cluttered fridge can lead to wasted food and make it difficult to find what you're looking for. Plus, a dirty fridge can harbor bacteria and odors that can affect the freshness of your food. So I've put together these useful fridge organization and cleaning hacks to help you keep your family fridge in top shape. By following these tips, you can save money, reduce food waste, and make sure that your food stays fresh and safe to eat.

Keep a "use first" section: Designate a section of your fridge for items that need to be used up soon, like leftovers or produce that's starting to go bad. This will help prevent food waste and ensure that you're eating the freshest food possible.

Use clear containers: Invest in clear containers to store your food in. This will make it easy to see what's inside and help you avoid forgotten leftovers.

Check the dates on your food. Throw out anything that is out of date.

Clean up spills immediately: If you spill something in your fridge, make sure to clean it up right away. This will prevent bacteria from growing and keep your fridge smelling fresh.

Use baking soda: Placing an open box of baking soda in your fridge can help absorb odors and keep your fridge smelling fresh.

Rotate your food: When you bring home groceries, make sure to rotate older items to the front so that they get used up first. This can help prevent food waste and ensure that you're eating the freshest food possible.

Deep clean your fridge regularly: It's important to deep clean your fridge every few months to prevent bacteria and odors from building up. Empty everything out, wipe down the shelves and walls with a mild cleaner, and toss any expired or old items.

Healthy eating

As a teenager, it's important to make healthy choices when it comes to what you eat. Your body is still growing and developing, and the foods you choose to eat can have a big impact on your health both now and in the future. From improving your physical health to setting a foundation for a healthier future, there are plenty of benefits to making healthy choices when it comes to what you eat.

So, let's dive in and explore some of the reasons why a healthy diet is so important for you.

Improved physical health

Eating a balanced and nutritious diet can help you maintain a healthy weight, improve your immune system, and reduce your risk of developing chronic diseases like diabetes and heart disease.

Increased energy and focus

Eating a healthy diet can provide your body with the nutrients it needs to keep you energized and focused throughout the day.

Better mood

Eating a healthy diet can improve your mood and reduce feelings of anxiety and depression.

Improved athletic performance

Eating a diet rich in nutrients can help you perform better in sports and other physical activities.

Better sleep

Eating a healthy diet can improve the quality of your sleep and help you wake up feeling refreshed.

Improved skin health

Eating a diet rich in fruits and vegetables can help improve your skin health and reduce the risk of acne and other skin problems.

Improved digestion

Eating a diet rich in fiber can improve your digestion and help avoid digestive problems.

Setting a healthy foundation for the future

By developing healthy eating habits as a teenager, you can set a foundation for a lifetime of healthy eating habits and a healthier future overall.

Easy meal ideas for teens

As a teenager, it can be tough to come up with meal ideas that are both easy to make and delicious. Here are 8 ideas to get you started:

Quesadillas

Grab some tortillas, cheese, and any other fillings you like (like chicken, vegetables, or beans) and cook them up in a pan for a quick and tasty meal.

Pasta with marinara sauce

Cook up your favorite pasta and top it with store-bought or homemade marinara sauce for an easy and satisfying meal.

Stir-fry

Toss some veggies, protein (like chicken, beef, or tofu), and rice or noodles in a wok or pan for a quick and healthy meal.

Sandwiches

Load up some bread with your favorite fillings (like turkey, cheese, lettuce, and tomato) for a quick and easy meal.

Tacos

Cook up some ground beef or chicken and load up some tortillas with all your favorite taco toppings for a fun and easy meal.

Grilled cheese

Make a classic grilled cheese sandwich by melting cheese between two slices of bread in a pan or on a griddle.

Smoothie bowls

Blend up some frozen fruit, yogurt, and milk to make a smoothie, then top it with granola, nuts, and fresh fruit for a delicious and healthy meal.

Baked potatoes

Bake a potato in the oven or microwave and top it with your favorite toppings (like cheese, sour cream, and chives) for a filling and easy meal.

These meals are all easy to make and can be customized with your favorite ingredients, so don't be afraid to get creative!

Plan & cook a meal

Planning and cooking a meal as a teenager can be a fun and rewarding experience. Here are some tips to help you get started:

Choose a recipe: Pick a recipe that sounds delicious and that you feel comfortable making. You can find recipes online, in cookbooks, or even ask your family or friends for recommendations.

Make a grocery list: Once you have your recipe, make a list of all the ingredients you'll need. Be sure to check your pantry and fridge first to see what you already have on hand.

Go shopping: Head to the grocery store and pick up everything on your list. If you're not sure where to find something, don't be afraid to ask an employee for help.

Prep your ingredients: Before you start cooking, take some time to prep your ingredients. Wash and chop any vegetables, measure out your spices, and get all your ingredients ready to go.

Follow the recipe: Follow the recipe carefully, and don't be afraid to ask for help if you're not sure about something. Take your time and read through the recipe before you start cooking.

Cook your meal: Use a timer to help you keep track of cooking times, and don't be afraid to taste your food as you go to make sure it's turning out the way you want it to.

Serve and enjoy: Once your meal is ready, plate it up and enjoy it with your family or friends. Congratulate yourself on a job well done!

Remember, cooking is a skill that takes practice, so don't get discouraged if your first few meals don't turn out perfectly. Just keep trying and have fun with it!

Table manners for teens

Good table manners are important for you for several reasons. Knowing how to behave at the table can give you confidence in social situations and make you feel more comfortable around others. Good table manners show respect for those around you, including your family, friends, and other guests. It demonstrates that you are considerate of others and their needs. In some situations, such as job interviews or business meetings, good table manners can make a positive impression on others and show that you are professional and capable. Good table manners are an important part of social etiquette and can have a positive impact on your personal and professional life. There is nothing worse than sitting beside someone who is talking and spitting their food onto your plate! Here are some tips to get you started.

Use utensils: Use a fork, knife, and spoon to eat your food, rather than your fingers. If you're not sure which utensil to use, start from the outside and work your way in.

Keep your elbows off the table: Resting your elbows on the table while you eat is considered rude. Keep your arms and hands in your lap or on the table.

Chew with your mouth closed: Avoid talking with your mouth full and make sure to chew your food with your mouth closed.

Take small bites: Taking smaller bites of food will help you chew and swallow more easily.

Wait your turn to speak: Don't interrupt others while they are speaking, and wait your turn to talk.

Say please and thank you: Remember to say "please" when asking for something and "thank you" when you receive it.

Don't reach over others: If you need something that's out of reach, politely ask someone to pass it to you rather than reaching over them.

Offer to help: When the meal is over, offer to help clear the dishes or clean up the table.

Vitamins & supplements

It's important to have a balanced and nutritious diet that provides all the necessary vitamins and minerals. However, there may be some situations where taking vitamins can be beneficial. Here are some examples:

Nutrient deficiencies: If a teenager has a nutrient deficiency, such as low iron or vitamin D levels, taking vitamins may be necessary to supplement their diet.

Restricted diets: If a teenager follows a restricted diet, such as a vegan or vegetarian diet, they may need to take vitamins to ensure they are getting enough of certain nutrients that are predominantly found in animal products.

Sports and physical activity: Teenagers who are highly active in sports or physical activity may need to take vitamins to support their increased nutrient needs and aid in recovery.

Health conditions: Teenagers with certain health conditions, such as celiac disease or Crohn's disease, may have difficulty absorbing certain vitamins and may need to take supplements to ensure they are getting enough.

In general, it's best for teenagers to get their vitamins and minerals from a balanced and varied diet. However, in certain situations, taking vitamins may be necessary to support their overall health and wellbeing. You need to talk to a nurse or doctor before you start taking any vitamins or supplements.

Exercise & health

Finding a new sport as a teenager can be an exciting and rewarding experience. Here are some ways you can find a sport that you'll enjoy:

1. Look up different sports online or in a sports store to see what catches your eye. Read about the rules, requirements, and equipment needed for each sport.
2. See what local clubs are in your area. Maybe you can find a local tennis, rugby, soccer, badminton, baseball or running club.
3. Ask your friends what sports they play and if they recommend any for you. You may discover a new interest that you both can enjoy together.
4. Attend local sporting events or games to see what sports you might enjoy. This can help you see the excitement and enthusiasm around the sport.
5. Try a variety of sports. Experiment with different sports by attending a few practices or games to get a feel for the sport. This can help you determine if the sport is right for you.
6. Choose a sport that suits your physical abilities and interests. For example, if you enjoy being in the water, try swimming or water polo.

7. Consider your goals for participating in a sport. Do you want to have fun, compete at a high level, or improve your physical fitness? This can help you choose a sport that aligns with your goals.

8. If you can find a sport that you will enjoy, you are much more likely to keep doing it!

Remember, finding a new sport should be a fun and exciting experience. Try new sports and challenge yourself to learn and grow in a new activity.

Walking 10k steps

Walking 10,000 steps a day is often recommended as a general guideline for overall health and wellness, including for teenagers. Let me explain why.

Physical health

Walking is great to help improve your heart health, strengthen your muscles and bones, and keep you feeling fit and healthy. These benefits can help reduce the risk of chronic conditions - like obesity, type 2 diabetes, and heart disease.

Mental health

Regular physical activity, including walking, can also have a positive impact on mental health. Walking can help you feel less stressed, improve your mood, and boost your self-esteem.

Academic performance

Studies have shown that physical activity can have a positive impact on academic performance. Walking 10,000 steps a day can improve your focus and attention span, which can lead to better academic performance.

Socialization

Walking can be a social activity that can help teenagers connect with friends, family, and their community. This can have a positive impact on mental health and social skills.

Developing healthy habits

Adding exercise into your daily routine, such as aiming for 10,000 steps a day, can help teenagers develop healthy habits that they can carry with them throughout their lives.

If 10,000 steps a day sounds like a lot for you, it's a good goal to strive for and can have numerous benefits for a teenager's overall health and wellbeing. You can use a tracker app on your phone to track your steps for you.

Yoga & pilates

Yoga and Pilates are both low-impact forms of exercise that can have numerous benefits for teenagers. Both yoga and Pilates can help improve flexibility, strength, balance, and posture. These benefits can help reduce the risk of injury and promote overall physical health.

Yoga and Pilates can also have a positive impact on mental health. Both practices incorporate breathing techniques and mindfulness, which can make you feel less stressed and anxious and improve your overall mental wellbeing. Yoga and Pilates can help teenagers become more aware of their bodies and how they move. This can help them develop better body awareness and control, which can have a positive impact on overall physical performance.

By improving flexibility and strength, yoga and Pilates can help reduce the risk of injury during other physical activities or sports. As teenagers navigate the challenges of adolescence, participating in yoga or Pilates can also help boost self-esteem and promote a positive body image.

Overall, incorporating yoga or Pilates into your weekly routine can have numerous physical and mental health benefits.

Sleep

Sleep is crucial for people of all ages, but it is especially important for teenagers as they undergo significant physical and emotional changes. Sleep helps the body repair and grow tissue, as well as strengthen the immune system. It also helps regulate hormones, which can impact growth and development. Getting enough sleep can improve mood and reduce stress and anxiety. In contrast, sleep deprivation can lead to irritability, depression, and other emotional problems. If you don't get a good night's sleep you can have trouble concentrating and retaining information, which can affect your school work.

Getting adequate sleep can also help improve memory and learning. Sleep is essential for physical recovery and can help improve athletic performance. Sleep deprivation can lead to slower reaction times, decreased endurance, and increased risk of injury. Teenagers who do not get enough sleep have a greater chance of being involved in car accidents due to decreased reaction time and impaired judgment.

Getting enough sleep is essential for teenagers to maintain physical and emotional well-being, academic and athletic performance, and overall safety. So it's worth making sure you are getting enough shut eye!

How much sleep do you need?

The amount of sleep a teenager needs can vary depending on their individual needs, but generally speaking, teenagers require about 8-10 hours of sleep per night. However, many teens do not get enough sleep due to factors such as academic and extracurricular demands, social activities, and electronic device use.

It's important for teens to prioritize getting enough sleep, as sleep deprivation can have negative impacts on their physical and emotional health, academic performance, and overall well-being. Starting to use a regular sleep schedule with a relaxing bedtime routine can help promote healthy sleep habits. Additionally, reducing screen time before bedtime and avoiding caffeine and sugary foods in the evening can also help improve sleep quality.

Meditation

Meditation can be beneficial for teenagers in many ways. It can help you manage stress and anxiety, improve focus and concentration, and promote overall mental and emotional well-being.

As teenagers navigate the challenges of school, social relationships, and personal growth, you may experience feelings of overwhelm, anxiety, or uncertainty. Meditation can help you develop the skills to manage these emotions and maintain a sense of calm and balance. By living in the present and adopting a non-judgmental awareness of their thoughts and feelings, you can learn to respond to stressors in a more constructive way.

Meditation is also known to have physical health benefits, such as reducing blood pressure and improving sleep quality. Adding meditation into your life can help you become more resilient, and improve your overall quality of life.

Smoking

Smoking is not a good idea, no matter what age you are. It's incredibly bad for your health. And not only that, but it's going to cause you years of issues. As a teen, you might have thought 'I'll start smoking' and it'll be fine.

The problem then arises a few months or years later, when you decide it costs way too much money, and you want to stop smoking for your health. It takes a huge amount of willpower and pain to stop smoking - and that's because smoking is addictive. Once you start smoking, your body will start to crave it. So you are just creating so much pain and heartache for yourself later in your life.

It's much less stress, less drama and miles better for your health, to just never start smoking. If you are someone who likes maximum results for minimum efforts, avoiding smoking is one of the most important things you can do as a teenager. Here are a few other downsides to smoking:

Cigarettes contain more than 7,000 chemicals, many of which are toxic and can cause serious health problems like heart disease, lung cancer, chronic bronchitis and emphysema.

Additionally, smoking can negatively affect your physical appearance. It can cause bad breath, yellowing of teeth, premature aging of skin, and hair loss.

Smoking is also expensive. The cost of cigarettes can quickly add up, taking away money that could be spent on other things such as hobbies, entertainment, or saving for the future.

Furthermore, smoking can have a negative impact on social relationships. Many people find the smell of smoke unpleasant, and it may be difficult to find friends who are comfortable around smokers.

Finally, quitting smoking is incredibly difficult. Nicotine is highly addictive, and the longer you smoke, the harder it is to quit. It's important to remember that not starting smoking in the first place is the best way to avoid the many negative consequences associated with smoking.

Drinking

Every country has its own legal age for drinking. So your first step is to make sure you know this. There is no need to break the law & end up in trouble.

Drinking alcohol can have serious negative effects on your body and how you feel, and even with your friends and school work.

Firstly, drinking can impair brain development, which continues into the mid-20s. This means that teenagers who drink heavily are at risk of having lifelong issues with memory, learning, and impulse control. Additionally, drinking can lead to poor decision-making, which can result in dangerous behavior such as drunk driving, unprotected sex, and drug use.

Drinking can also have negative physical health effects, such as liver damage, heart disease, and an increased risk of certain cancers. It can also negatively affect a teenager's mental health, increasing the likelihood of depression, anxiety, and suicide.

Furthermore, drinking can have negative social consequences for teenagers, such as strained relationships with friends and family, problems at school or work, and even legal troubles. The risks associated with underage drinking are simply not worth it. There are many serious potential consequences of drinking and so it's important for you to make healthy and responsible choices for themselves.

Drugs

Substance abuse can be a serious problem for teenagers, which is why avoiding drugs in your teenage years is so important. Taking drugs can literally rob you of your future. Here are some reasons why.

Addiction: Using drugs as a teenager can quickly lead to addiction. Once someone becomes addicted, it can be incredibly difficult to stop using.

Health problems: Substance abuse can cause a variety of health problems, from lung damage to liver failure to heart disease. These health problems can be difficult to treat and can even be life-threatening.

Mental health issues: Drug use can also lead to mental health issues such as depression, anxiety, and psychosis. These issues can really affect a teenager's quality of life.

Legal problems: Using drugs is illegal, and getting caught can result in legal problems, including fines and even jail time.

Negative impact on relationships: Substance abuse can have a negative impact on a teenager's relationships with friends and family. It can be difficult for loved ones to watch someone they care about struggle with addiction.

Poor academic performance: Drug use can lead to poor academic performance, which can have long-lasting effects on a teenager's future opportunities.

If you're struggling with drug addiction as a teenager, it's important to know that you're not alone and that there are many resources available to help you. Here are some ideas:

Talk to someone you trust: It could be a parent, teacher, or counselor. Talking about your struggles can help you feel less alone and get the support you need.

Seek professional help: There are many professionals who specialize in treating drug addiction, such as doctors, therapists, and addiction specialists. They can offer you personalized treatment and support.

Join a support group: These groups can offer you a sense of community and help you stay accountable to your recovery goals.

Remember, overcoming drug addiction is not easy, but it is possible. With the right support and resources, you can beat addiction and live a healthy, fulfilling life.

First aid & emergencies

First aid is an important skill that everyone should know, including teenagers. Knowing what to do when someone is not well can even save a life. Here are some tips on first aid for teenagers.

First and foremost, always call for emergency medical services (EMS) immediately in a life-threatening situation, such as someone not breathing, having a heart attack or stroke, or a severe injury. Do not try to handle the situation alone.

However, there are still many situations where basic first aid can help. For example, if someone has a minor cut or scrape, you can clean the wound and cover it with a sterile bandage. Here are some other tips:

- If someone is choking, encourage them to cough and try to remove the blockage by giving them back blows or performing the Heimlich maneuver if necessary.
- If you see someone having a seizure, try to keep them safe by moving any sharp or hard objects away from them and placing something soft under their head. Do not try to hold them down or put anything in their mouth.

- If someone has a sprain or strain, use the RICE method: rest, ice, compression, and elevation. Rest the affected area, apply ice to reduce swelling, wrap the area with a bandage for compression, and elevate the affected limb above the heart if possible.
- If someone is having an allergic reaction, use an EpiPen if available and call for medical assistance immediately.
- If someone is experiencing a nosebleed, have them sit down and lean their head forward slightly. Pinch the soft part of their nose with your fingers for 10-15 minutes until the bleeding stops.

Remember, first aid is not the same level of care as from a nurse or doctor, but it can provide fast help and possibly prevent further harm until medical assistance arrives. You can take a first aid course to learn more about how to respond in different situations.

Personal health & grooming

Personal health and grooming are hugely important as they contribute significantly to our overall physical, emotional, and social well-being. Practicing good personal hygiene, such as regular showers or baths, brushing teeth, and wearing clean clothes, keeps us clean and fresh-smelling. It also helps us feel good about ourselves and boosts our self-confidence.

Skin care

As a teenager, it's important to take care of your skin to keep it healthy and glowing. With so many skin care products and routines out there, how do you know where to start? But don't worry, I'm here to help! We'll go over some simple but effective skin care tips that you can easily incorporate into your daily routine. Whether you're dealing with acne or just want to maintain healthy skin, these tips are perfect for all teenagers.

Cleanse your face twice a day: Use a gentle cleanser. This takes off dirt, oil, and makeup from your face in the morning and before bed.

Moisturize regularly: Keeping your skin hydrated is important for maintaining its health and preventing dryness and breakouts. Use a light, oil-free moisturizer daily.

Wear sunscreen: Keep your skin safe from harmful UV rays by wearing sunscreen. You need to do this every day, even on cloudy days.

Don't touch your face: Your hands carry bacteria that can cause breakouts, so avoid touching your face or picking at pimples.

Avoid harsh products: Avoid using harsh scrubs or astringents that can damage your skin and strip it of natural oils.

Get enough sleep: Not getting enough sleep can leave you feeling stressed. This can lead to breakouts and other skin problems. Try to get at least 8 hours of sleep every night.

Stay hydrated: Drinking lots of water is a great way to flush toxins out of your body and keeps your skin looking healthy.

Eat a healthy diet: Eating lots of fruits, vegetables, and whole grains can help keep your skin healthy too.

Dealing with acne

Experiencing acne breakouts can be frustrating and sometimes affect your self-confidence. Acne is a very common teenage skin condition, caused by the overproduction of oil and dead skin cells clogging pores. While you might try and pop pimples or use harsh products, there are several ways to help manage and reduce acne without damaging your skin. Here are some tips and advice on how to help teenagers deal with acne in a healthy and effective way.

Develop a consistent skincare routine: Wash your face every day with a cleanser suitable for teenage skin and use a moisturizer that does not contain ingredients which will block the pores on your skin.

Avoid touching your face: Picking, squeezing or touching your pimples can worsen acne and spread bacteria.

Keep your hair off your face: Hair products can also cause acne, so avoid using oily hair products and keep your hair off your face. Don't use a lot of conditioner on your hair, as that can drip onto your upper back and cause skin issues also if you don't rinse it all off.

Don't share makeup: Sharing makeup can transfer bacteria and cause breakouts, so avoid sharing makeup with friends.

Wear sunscreen: Sun damage can worsen acne, so make sure to use a sunscreen that does not contain ingredients which will block the pores on your skin daily.

Watch your diet: Certain foods like dairy, sugar, and greasy foods can cause acne, so try to eat a balanced diet.

Manage stress: Stress can worsen acne, so try to manage stress through exercise, meditation, or other relaxation techniques.

Seek help from a dermatologist: If over-the-counter treatments don't work, consider seeing a dermatologist who can recommend prescription treatments tailored to your skin type and acne severity.

Hair

Taking care of your hair can really affect how you look and feel. Whether you have long, short, curly or straight hair, there are things you can do to keep it healthy and looking its best. Here are some hair tips for teens to help you achieve your best hair yet:

Wash your hair regularly: Wash your hair at least twice a week to remove dirt and oil buildup. If you have very oily hair, you may need to wash it more often.

Use the right shampoo and conditioner: Choose a shampoo and conditioner that is right for your hair type. If you have dry hair, use a moisturizing shampoo and conditioner. If you have oily hair, use a clarifying shampoo.

Avoid using hot tools too often: Curling irons, straighteners, and blow dryers can damage your hair if you use them too often. Use heat protectant products when you do use them.

Brush your hair gently: Use a wide-tooth comb or brush to detangle your hair gently. Start at the ends of your hair, then your way upwards to prevent breakage.

Avoid tight hairstyles: Tight hairstyles like ponytails and braids can cause damage to your hair and scalp. Experiment with wearing it down or in loose hairstyles.

Keep your hair safe from the sun: The sun's UV rays can damage your hair just like it can damage your skin. Wear a hat to protect your hair when you're outside.

Eat healthy food: If you can eat a balanced diet with plenty of vitamins and minerals, this can help keep your hair healthy and strong.

Trim your hair regularly: Trimming your hair every 8 weeks can help prevent split ends and keep your hair looking healthy.

Remember, taking care of your hair doesn't have to be complicated. With these simple tips, you can keep your hair looking great and feeling healthy.

Teeth

Your teeth are incredibly important, so here are some trips to keep them in great shape.

Brush your teeth twice a day: This would be for at least two minutes, twice a day, with a fluoride toothpaste.

Floss daily: Flossing will take away plaque and food particles that get stuck between your teeth and under your gum line.

Use mouthwash to kill bacteria: Mouthwash can also help to freshen your breath.

Reduce or stop drinking & eating sugary and acidic foods and drinks: These types of foods and drinks can erode your tooth enamel and cause cavities.

Use a mouthguard: If you play sports or participate in activities that could injure your teeth, wear a mouthguard to protect them.

Visit the dentist regularly: Schedule regular dental checkups and cleanings to maintain good oral health and catch any issues early.

Don't use tobacco: Smoking or using other forms of tobacco can stain your teeth, cause bad breath, and increase your risk of oral cancer.

Do you grind your teeth? If do, ask your dentist about getting a mouth guard to prevent damage to your teeth.

Clothes

Clothes shopping

We all need clothes! Shopping for clothes as a teen is quite important. You're developing your own style, usually on a budget. Here are some tips to buy clothes as a teenager.

Set a budget: Before you start shopping, decide how much money you can afford to spend on clothes. This will help you avoid overspending and make sure you don't end up with items you can't afford.

Make a list: Make a list of the items you need before you start shopping. This will help you stay focused and avoid buying items you don't need.

Shop for basics: Invest in basic items that you can mix and match, such as t-shirts, jeans, and leggings. These items can be dressed up or down and are versatile.

Try everything on: It's important to try on clothes before you buy them, especially if you're buying from a new store or trying a new brand. This will help you make sure the clothes fit well and look good on you.

Consider quality: When buying clothes, think about the quality of the fabric and the construction. Quality clothes may cost more, but they will last longer and be a better value in the long run.

Think about the season: Consider the season when buying clothes. In the winter, you'll need warm clothes, while in the summer, you'll need clothes that are cool and breathable.

Don't be swayed by trends: While it's fun to follow fashion trends, don't be swayed by them if they don't suit your personal style. Stick to what makes you feel comfortable and confident.

Shop sales: Look for sales and discounts when shopping for clothes. You can often find great deals on clothes if you shop at the right time. Just make sure you don't buy something just because it's on sale if you don't really need it.

Taking care of your clothes

Taking care of your clothes is an essential part of maintaining a good wardrobe. As a teenager, you might not think too much about it, but knowing how to take care of your clothes properly can help them last longer and save you money in the long run. Here are some tips to help you take care of your clothes:

Read the labels: Always check the care labels on your clothes before washing them. Different fabrics require different care, so it's important to follow the instructions on the label.

Sort your laundry: Separate your clothes by color and fabric before washing them. This will prevent colors from bleeding and fabrics from getting damaged.

Use the right detergent: Use a detergent that's appropriate for the type of fabric you're washing. For example, use a gentle detergent for delicate fabrics.

Wash in cold water: Washing your clothes in cold water will help preserve their color and prevent shrinkage.

Don't overload the washing machine: Overloading the washing machine can damage your clothes and prevent them from getting clean. Follow the manufacturer's instructions for the maximum load size.

Hang dry: Avoid using the dryer for clothes that can shrink or lose their shape. Instead, hang them to dry.

Iron properly: If you need to iron your clothes, use the appropriate heat setting and be careful not to burn the fabric.

Store your clothes properly: Fold or hang your clothes neatly in your closet or dresser to prevent wrinkles and damage.

By following these tips, you can take care of your clothes and keep them looking great for longer.

Confidence & self-esteem

Mindset

A positive mindset is important as it can have a significant impact on our overall well-being, both now and in the future. When we have a positive mindset, we are more likely to feel happy and content with our lives. We may also be better able to cope with stress, anxiety, and other mental health issues.

Having a positive outlook can also help us build stronger relationships with others. Positive people are often more approachable and enjoyable to be around, which can help us form deeper connections with our friends, family members, and others in their lives.

Life can be unpredictable and challenging, especially during the teenage years. A positive mindset can help teens build resilience and bounce back from setbacks and difficulties.

Research has shown that students with a positive mindset tend to perform better academically than those with a negative mindset. By believing in ourselves and our abilities, teens may be more motivated to learn and succeed in school.

Overall, a positive mindset can help teenagers feel happier, more confident, and more fulfilled in their lives. It can also have a ripple effect, improving their relationships, academic performance, and future prospects. Here are some mindset strategies that can help you.

Focus on the good

Try to focus on the positive aspects of your life, rather than dwelling on the negative. You can do this by writing down things you are grateful for each day, or simply taking time to appreciate the good things in your life.

Practice self-care

Taking care of your mind and body can be a great way to promote positivity. Make sure to get enough sleep, eat healthy foods, and exercise regularly. You can also try meditation or deep breathing exercises to help reduce stress.

Surround yourself with positive people

Spending time with people who are positive and supportive can help you feel more optimistic about life. Seek out friends who lift you up and avoid those who bring you down.

Set goals

Setting goals and working towards them can help give you a sense of purpose and accomplishment. Make sure your goals are realistic and achievable, and celebrate your progress along the way.

Practice positive self-talk

The way you talk to yourself can have a big impact on your mindset. Try to replace negative self-talk with positive affirmations, such as "I am capable" or "I can do this." instead of saying 'I can't do this' say 'I haven't done this yet'.

Take time for yourself

It's important to take breaks and do things you enjoy. Whether it's reading a book, watching a movie, or spending time outdoors, make sure to take time for yourself and engage in activities that bring you joy.

Remember, maintaining a positive mindset takes practice and patience. It's okay to have bad days or negative thoughts, but by focusing on the good and taking care of yourself, you can cultivate a more positive outlook on life.

Dealing with stress & anxiety

It's completely normal to feel stressed or anxious from time to time, but it's important to understand what these feelings are and how to cope with them.

Stress is a physical and emotional response to a challenging situation, such as a big test or a difficult conversation with a friend. Anxiety, on the other hand, is a feeling of fear, worry, or unease about something that may or may not happen in the future.

Both stress and anxiety can affect your mood, your physical health, and your ability to concentrate. They can also lead to other issues such as insomnia, digestive problems, and a weakened immune system. The good news is that there are many ways to manage stress and anxiety. Here are some tips:

Practice relaxation techniques

Deep breathing, meditation, and yoga are all great ways to help reduce stress and anxiety. Find a technique that works for you and practice it regularly, even if it's just for a few minutes each day.

Stay active

Exercise is a great way to relieve stress and boost your mood. Try to get at least 30 minutes of physical activity each day, whether it's going for a walk, playing a sport, or dancing to your favorite music.

Connect with others

Talking to someone you really trust can be a great way to alleviate stress and anxiety. Talk to someone in your family, a friend, school counselor and share how you're feeling.

Avoid unhealthy coping mechanisms

While you may think in the short term turning to drugs, alcohol, or other unhealthy behaviors to cope with stress is a good idea, these habits can actually make the problem worse in the long run. Instead, try to find healthy ways to manage your emotions.

Get enough sleep

Lack of sleep can contribute to stress and anxiety. Try to get enough sleep each night and establish a bedtime routine to help you relax and unwind.

Practice self-care

Taking care of yourself is crucial for managing stress and anxiety.

Stress

Sometimes stress can be the result of ignoring something in your life. Is there an underlying issue in your life that is causing your stress? Can you get help to deal with it?

Make sure to eat a healthy diet, stay hydrated, and take breaks to do things you enjoy. You could play tennis, read a book, watch a movie, or spend time outdoors. Remember, everyone experiences stress and anxiety at times, and it's okay to ask for help.

Communicate your way out of trouble

Communicating effectively can be a useful tool for navigating challenging situations and avoiding trouble. Here are some tips for teenagers on how to communicate their way out of trouble:

Stay calm

When you're in a difficult situation, it's important to stay calm and collected. Take a moment and try not to react impulsively.

Listen actively

When someone is upset with you, it can be tempting to tune them out or get defensive. However, actively listening to their concerns and acknowledging their feelings can help de-escalate the situation.

Take responsibility

If you've made a mistake or contributed to the problem, own up to it. Apologize and try to make things right.

Be respectful

Even if you disagree with someone, it's important to treat them with respect. Avoid name-calling or attacking them personally.

Use "I" statements

When expressing your own feelings or concerns, use "I" statements rather than blaming or accusing the other person. For example, say "I feel hurt when you ignore me" instead of "You always ignore me."

Brainstorm solutions

Once you've both had a chance to share your perspectives, work together to come up with a solution that works for everyone involved.

Seek help if necessary

If you're struggling to communicate effectively or feel like you're in over your head, don't be afraid to seek help from a trusted adult, such as a parent, teacher, or counselor.

Remember, effective communication takes practice and patience. By staying calm, listening actively, and treating others with respect, you can navigate difficult situations and communicate your way out of trouble.

Useful phrases for tricky situations

Here are some useful phrases for teenagers to use in challenging high-pressure situations to help them stand up for themselves:

"I understand your perspective, but I have a different point of view."

This phrase can be helpful when someone is pressuring you to do something that you're not comfortable with. It acknowledges the other person's perspective while also asserting your own boundaries.

"Can we take a break from this conversation? I need time to think about it."

You can take a step back from a high-pressure situation to gather your thoughts and emotions. This phrase can help you assert your need for space while also keeping the conversation open for later.

"I don't feel comfortable doing that."

If someone is pressuring you to do something that goes against your values or makes you uncomfortable, it's important to assert your boundaries. This phrase can help you communicate your discomfort in a clear and direct way.

"I appreciate your concern, but I can handle this on my own."

Sometimes, well-meaning friends or family members can add to the pressure of a situation. This phrase can help you communicate that you appreciate their concern, but that you have the ability to handle the situation on your own.

"I need to take care of myself right now."

Your mental and emotional well-being should always come first. This phrase can help you assert your need for self-care and set boundaries when you're feeling overwhelmed.

Remember, it's okay to assert yourself and stand up for your own needs and boundaries. By using clear and direct language, you can communicate your perspective and take control of high-pressure situations.

"Do not speak to me like that"

This phrase is a clear and direct way to assert your boundaries and communicate that you will not tolerate being spoken to in a way that is hurtful, aggressive, or demeaning.

"I'm not finished speaking"

This phrase can help you assert your right to be heard and communicate that you need the other person to listen to what you have to say.

"I'm not obligated to explain myself to you"

It's ok to assert yourself also when someone is asking you personal or sensitive questions that you don't feel comfortable answering. It's important to set boundaries and protect your privacy, especially when someone is being nosy or invasive.

"I'm not taking feedback on this"

When you have made a decision or taken action that you feel confident about, and you don't want to receive unsolicited feedback or criticism, this is a useful reply.

"My weight is not up for discussion"

It's important to remember that everyone's body is unique and that weight should never be a topic of conversation without consent. When someone is making comments about your weight, body shape, or appearance in a way that is inappropriate or hurtful, go ahead and ask them to stop.

"No is my answer"

It's important to remember that you have the right to say no and set boundaries, even if it disappoints or upsets others. What you need and feel is just as important as anyone else, and it's okay to prioritize them.

"I have the right to be treated with respect"

Everyone deserves to be treated with dignity and respect, regardless of the situation. It's important to assert yourself and communicate that you will not tolerate behavior that is hurtful or inappropriate.

Social media health check

Stay safe online & things to avoid

The internet has become a normal part of our lives, and teens are spending more time online than ever before. While the internet can be useful for information and entertainment, it also comes with certain risks and dangers.

It's important to stay safe online for several reasons. First and foremost, the internet is not always a safe place. There are cyberbullies, scammers, and predators who may try to take advantage of young people online. If we are not careful we may be exposed to inappropriate content, or they may accidentally download malware or viruses that can harm our devices.

In addition to the risks associated with internet use, there are also potential long-term consequences to consider. Anything that is posted online can potentially be seen by anyone, now or in the future. This means that a post or message that seems harmless now could have serious repercussions down the road, such as impacting college admissions or future employment opportunities.

To stay safe online, you should take steps to protect their privacy and personal information, avoid interactions with strangers, and be careful about what you post online.

By staying safe online, we can enjoy the benefits of the internet without putting themselves at risk. We can connect with friends and family, explore their interests, and learn new things, all while staying safe and secure online. Here are some tips to stay safe online:

Protect your personal information

Be careful about sharing personal information such as your full name, address, phone number, or any other identifying details online. Avoid posting sensitive information on social media, and make sure your privacy settings are very strong and only your friends that you know in real life can see your information.

Be cautious with strangers

Never meet up with someone you have met online without first getting permission from a parent or guardian, and always meet in a public place with plenty of people around. Be careful about sharing personal information or photos with people you don't know in real life.

Think before you post

Remember that anything you post online can potentially be seen by anyone, now or in the future. Avoid posting anything that you wouldn't want your parents, teachers, or future employers to see. Be respectful and responsible with your online behavior.

Use strong passwords

Use long, complicated and different passwords for all of your online accounts, and change them regularly. Don't use the same password for multiple accounts.

Be aware of cyberbullying

Cyberbullying is a serious problem, and it's important to know how to recognize it and how to handle this situation – if it happens to you or a friend of yours. Don't respond to cyberbullies or retaliate, and always tell a trusted adult if you or someone you know is being targeted.

Use parental controls

If you're under 18, consider using parental controls on your devices and apps to limit access to inappropriate content and ensure that you're following safe online practices.

By following these tips, you can stay safe and responsible online, and avoid the risks and dangers associated with internet use. Remember, staying safe online is everyone's responsibility, and it's important to be aware of potential risks.

Social media - creator or consumer?

Are you an online content creator or consumer?

An online content producer is someone who creates and shares content online, such as videos, blog posts, podcasts, social media posts, or other digital media. They use various tools and platforms to create and distribute their content, with the goal of engaging with their audience and building a following. Examples of online content producers include vloggers, bloggers, podcasters, social media influencers, and digital marketers. Quite often a content producer is also running an online business of some sort. Perhaps they are sharing pictures of the candles they are making and selling on Instagram. Or they are earning money by making videos on makeup techniques.

On the other hand, an online content consumer is someone who consumes and interacts with online content, but does not necessarily create their own. They may watch videos, read blog posts or articles, listen to podcasts, follow social media accounts, or engage with online communities. Examples of online content consumers include social media users, online shoppers, news readers, and entertainment consumers.

Online content producers are actively creating and sharing content - usually to grow a business of some type to better their finances and lives, while online content consumers are passively consuming it. They are spending hours of their life every day, watching videos and making money for other people.

Ideally, you would want to keep your online content consumer time to a minimum each day, as there is little to no benefit in it.

Spending a lot of time online can be bad for our physical and mental health, as well as our social and academic lives. Social media is that it can be addictive, leading to excessive use and neglect of other important activities, such as exercise, sleep, and face-to-face social interaction. This can cause a lot of health problems, including obesity, cardiovascular disease, and diabetes.

In addition to the physical effects, excessive social media use can also have negative impacts on teens' mental health. Social media can be a source of stress, anxiety, and depression, particularly if teenagers are constantly comparing themselves to others and seeking validation through likes, comments, and followers.

Cyberbullying is also a serious problem on social media, which can cause emotional distress and even lead to suicide in extreme cases. Moreover, spending too much time on social media can affect teenagers' academic performance, as it can lead to procrastination, distraction, and lack of focus. It can also interfere with their sleep patterns, which can further exacerbate these problems.

So while social media can be a useful tool for communication, entertainment, and self-expression, it is important to be mindful of our social media consumer use and to maintain a healthy balance between online and offline activities.

Track your time spent & set new habit goals

Tracking your time spent on social media can be an important first step in reducing your social media use and maintaining a healthy balance between online and offline activities. Here are some tips for how to track your time spent on social media:

Use a time tracking app

There are many apps available that can track your time spent on various apps and websites, including social media platforms.

Set a timer

Another simple way to track your time spent on social media is to set a timer each time you use a social media app or website. Now you can become more aware of how much time you are spending on social media and encourage you to use it more intentionally.

Keep a journal

You can also track your time spent on social media by keeping a journal or log of your social media use. This can be as simple as jotting down the time and duration of each social media session in a notebook or on your phone.

Use your phone's screen time feature

Many smartphones have built-in screen time features so you can see how long you are spending on various apps and websites. Check your phone's settings to see if this feature is available and how to access it.

By tracking your time spent on social media, you can become more aware of your habits and see where you may need to make changes. You can then use this information to set goals for reducing your social media use.

Healthy social media habits

Here are some healthy social media habits that teenagers can practice to maintain a healthy balance between online and offline activities:

Set limits

It's important to set limits on the amount of time spent on social media each day. This can be done by using a timer, setting screen time limits on your device, or scheduling specific times for social media use.

Take breaks

Taking regular breaks from social media can help reduce stress and anxiety. You can do this by taking short breaks during the day or even taking a break from social media for a day or two each week.

Practice mindfulness

Deep breathing and meditation can really help you feel better, reduce stress and increase your focus. This can be especially helpful when using social media to avoid getting caught up in negative interactions or feelings of envy.

Use social media for positive interactions

Focus on using social media for positive interactions, such as connecting with friends and family, learning new things, or engaging with positive communities. Avoid using social media for negative interactions, such as cyberbullying or engaging in arguments.

Be aware of your emotions

Be aware of how social media makes you feel and take steps to address negative emotions. If social media is causing stress or anxiety, take a break or seek support from a trusted friend or family member.

Engage in offline activities

Make sure to engage in a variety of offline activities, such as exercise, hobbies, and spending time with friends and family. This can help maintain a healthy balance between online and offline activities.

Remember, social media can be a valuable tool for communication and self-expression, but it's important to practice healthy habits to maintain a positive and fulfilling online experience.

Money, budgeting, side hustle, volunteering

Pocket money

Pocket money is an important aspect of growing up and learning how to manage money. As a teenager, having pocket money can give you a sense of independence and help you learn the value of money. However, it can also be easy to spend it all at once or not manage it wisely.

Let's look at some ways you can manage your pocket money responsibly. These tips can help you make your money last longer and achieve your financial goals, whether it's saving for something special or just making sure that you can meet your regular expenses. So let's dive in!

Create a budget

It's important to create a budget and track your spending to make sure you're not spending too much, and that you can make your money last. Make a list of your regular expenses, such as transportation or snacks, and decide how much you want to spend on each category.

Set savings goals

It's important to save some of your pocket money for future expenses or to achieve a specific goal. This can be done by setting savings goals and putting aside a certain amount of money each week or month.

Avoid impulse buying

It's easy to buy something on a whim. Try to avoid impulse buying by taking a few moments to think before making a purchase. Do you really need the item? Or is it something that you can do without?

Look for deals

Keep an eye out for special deals and discounts when shopping for items to make your money go further. Try shopping at thrift stores or secondhand shops to find quality items at a lower cost.

Earn extra money

If you're looking to make extra money, consider doing odd jobs or offering your skills to others. This can include babysitting, pet sitting, or tutoring.

Be responsible

Remember to be responsible with your pocket money and not to spend it all at once. It's important to manage your money wisely to ensure that you can meet your needs and save for the future.

By following these tips, teens can learn to manage their pocket money rcsponsibly and set themselves up for financial success in the future.

Get a part-time job

There are several reasons why you could consider getting a part-time job. Firstly, having a part-time job can provide you with valuable work experience that they can use in the future. This can help them build your resumes, develop important skills, and gain a better understanding of the working world.

Secondly, earning your own money can give you a sense of independence and responsibility. It can help you learn to manage their finances, become more self-sufficient and even save for college.

Thirdly, a part-time job can teach you important life skills such as time management, communication, and teamwork. These skills can be applied to your academic and personal lives as well. Additionally, a part-time job can expose you to new people and experiences, helping you to grow as individuals and broaden their horizons.

There are many types of part-time jobs that are suitable for teenagers. Here are a few examples:

Retail or food service: Jobs at stores or restaurants are common options for teens. They may include tasks such as cashiering, stocking, or serving customers.

Babysitting or pet sitting: Teens can offer their services to families in need of childcare or pet care. These jobs may require some prior experience or training, but they can be rewarding and flexible.

Tutoring or teaching assistance: Teens can offer their academic skills to others by tutoring or assisting teachers at their school or local learning centers.

Lawn care or landscaping: Teens can offer their services to neighbors or local businesses by mowing lawns, trimming bushes, or landscaping.

Dog walking or pet sitting: Many pet owners need help with walking their dogs or taking care of their pets while they are away.

Car washing or detailing: Offering car washing or detailing services could be a great way for teens to earn money.

Lifeguarding: Teens can work as a lifeguard at a community pool or beach, which requires some training but can be a great way to earn money and stay active.

It's important to find a job that matches your skills and interests, and also consider your schedule and availability. With some effort and persistence, you can find a part-time job that is rewarding, fun, and helps them learn new skills.

Start a business

Perhaps you want to earn some money, but you have an idea that you would love to start a business. Well why not! It's a great idea. And there are so many opportunities.

Here are some online business startup ideas that could be great for aspiring entrepreneurs:

1. Social media marketing: Many businesses need help with managing their social media accounts, creating content, and reaching new customers. If you love a certain social media platform, you could offer your services to a local business who needs help managing that platform.
2. Graphic design services: Graphic designers can offer their services to businesses and individuals who need logos, website designs, and other visual assets. If you have skills with a graphic design software or platform, this could be perfect for you.
3. Arts and crafts sales: Teens who are skilled in creating handmade crafts or artwork can sell their creations online or at local markets.
4. Write and publish books online.
5. Design and publish smartphone apps online.
6. Sell an online course.
7. Start a handmade jewelry business.
8. Start an online custom wedding invitations design business.

9. Start a business making soaps, lotions, and lip balms.

10. There is a growing market for handmade and unique pet supplies, such as dog collars, cat toys, and pet beds.

These are just a few ideas to get started with. With some research, creativity, and hard work, entrepreneurs can find many opportunities to start their own successful online businesses.

Guide to credit cards for teens

Credit cards are a way to borrow money from a bank or credit card company in order to buy something. Usually you have to be 18 years of age to get a credit card.

This is how they work:

With a credit card you are actually borrowing money from the credit card company, which you then need to pay back over time.

You will have a maximum amount of money you can borrow using the card each month. When you make a purchase, the amount you spend is added to your credit card balance. Each month, you will receive a statement that shows your balance, the minimum payment due, and the due date when you have to pay back the money.

If you don't pay off all the money you owe on the credit card by the due date, you will start to accrue interest on the amount you owe. The interest rate can vary a lot. Most interest rates are very high which is very bad for you. Some credit cards also come with additional fees, such as an annual fee or a fee for balance transfers.

The dangers of credit cards

While credit cards can be a helpful financial tool, there are also potential dangers to be aware of. Here are some of the problems with credit cards:

High-interest debt

If you don't pay off your credit card balance in full each month, you will start to accrue interest on the amount you owe. Credit card interest rates can be quite high, and if you carry a balance over a long period of time, you can end up paying a lot in interest charges.

Overspending

It can be easy to spend more than you planned to, when you have a credit card, especially if you have a high credit limit. You can quickly find yourself in debt. You need to avoid this at all costs.

Fees

Some credit cards come with fees, such as an annual fee, a fee for balance transfers, or a fee for going over your credit limit. These fees can add up quickly and make it more difficult to pay off your balance.

Credit score damage

If you miss a credit card payment or carry a high balance on your card, it can negatively impact your credit score. This can make it harder to get approved for loans or credit in the future.

Fraud and identity theft

Using credit cards online or in stores can make you more vulnerable to fraud and identity theft. It's important to monitor your credit card statements regularly and report any unauthorized charges to your credit card company immediately.

When you are getting a credit card, always pay off 100% of the amount you owe, every single month. So your card balance goes back to 0 each month. Never owe money on your credit card company, as the interest rates are very high and it is much more difficult to pay the money back later on.

The dangers of debt

The golden rule is to avoid debt (loans of any sort) as much as you can. If you are in debt, do everything you can to pay it back as fast as possible.

Debt can be a serious problem for many people, especially if it starts to spiral out of control. Here are some of the dangers of debt:

High-interest rates

Many types of debt, such as credit cards or payday loans, come with high-interest rates. If you can't pay off your debt quickly, you can end up paying a lot in interest charges over time.

Damage to credit score

If you miss your credit card payments, it can damage your credit score. This can make it harder to get approved for loans or credit in the future, or lead to higher interest rates on any credit you do receive.

Stress and anxiety

Debt can cause a lot of stress and anxiety. If you're constantly worried about how you're going to pay your bills, it can take a toll on your mental health and your physical health too.

Limited financial options

If you're carrying a lot of debt, it can limit your financial options. You may not be able to save for emergencies or retirement, or you may have to put off major purchases or life events, such as buying a home or starting a family.

Collection actions

If you fall behind on your debt payments, you may start receiving calls and letters from debt collectors. They may even take legal action against you, such as garnishing your wages or putting a lien on your property.

Student loans

Student loans are a way to finance your education if you don't have the money to pay for it up front. It's important to remember that student loans are a serious financial commitment and should be approached with care. Before taking out any loans, make sure you understand the terms and conditions and have a plan for repaying them after graduation.

I would always focus my energy on asking myself how can I create more income. Perhaps you still need the loan, but you get a part-time job so you can pay the loan back faster. Or you start a business 12 months before you know you'll need the loan, so you can earn the money in advance and then apply for a smaller loan.

What to never borrow money for

There are many things that it is never wise to borrow money for, or go into debt on your credit card for. Here are a few examples:

Non-essential expenses

It's never a good idea to borrow money for non-essential expenses, such as a luxury vacation or a new wardrobe. If you can't afford it, it's best to save up for it instead of putting it on credit.

High-risk investments

Investing can help you to grow your wealth, but it's important to do so wisely and slowly. Borrowing money to invest in high-risk ventures, such as stocks or cryptocurrencies, is generally not a good idea.

Day-to-day expenses

If you're having trouble making ends meet and need to borrow money to pay for basic expenses like groceries or rent, it's a sign that you need to reassess your budget and slow down your spending.

Repaying other debt

Taking out a loan to pay off other debt may seem like a good idea, but it can actually make your financial situation worse if you're not careful. You could end up with even more debt if you're not able to keep up with the new loan payments.

Risky business ventures

Starting a new business can be a great idea, but if you're thinking about borrowing money to start it, make sure you know what you're doing. These days, there are thousands of businesses you can start for very little money.

Remember, borrowing money is a serious financial decision that should not be taken lightly. It's important to think carefully about why you need to borrow money and whether it's a wise financial decision before you take on any debt.

Getting your first car

Buying your first car is a huge milestone, but it can also be overwhelming. Here are some handy tips:

Determine your budget

Before you start looking at cars, it's important to determine how much you can spend. This will help you choose the right car and prevent you from overspending.

Decide what you need

Think about what you'll be using the car for and what features are important to you. Do you need a car with good mileage? Are you looking for something with plenty of storage space? Do you need a car with four-wheel drive for snowy winters? Once you know what you're looking for, start researching cars that fit your criteria. Look up reviews online and ask friends and family for recommendations.

Test drive

Always test drive a car before you buy it. You can see how it handles and whether it's comfortable for you to drive, and if it makes any odd noises.

Get a car inspection

Before you buy your car, ask a mechanic to look at it. This can help you identify any potential issues with the car and prevent you from buying a lemon.

Negotiate

It's ok to negotiate the price of the car. Do your research ahead of time so you know what a fair price is for the car you're interested in.

Consider financing options

If you're not able to pay for the car in cash, you'll need to consider financing options. Shop around for the best interest rates and read the full terms of the loan. It's way better to pay cash for a less fancy car, than to buy a fancy car and go into debt. So avoid debt as much as you can.

Don't forget about insurance

When you buy a new car you'll need to have insurance ready. Shop around for the best rates and make sure you have the coverage you need.

Buying your first car can be a bit intimidating, but if you take your time and do your research, you can find a car that fits your needs and your budget.

Driver's license & rules of the road

In most countries, in order to drive a car you need to apply for a driving license. The age you can do this will vary. Once you are old enough, check out the requirements and submit your paperwork. Often you'll need to pass a written test on the rules of the road and basic driving skills. You'll also need to pass a vision test.

Some states & countries require that you complete a driver's education course before you can apply for a license. This course typically includes both classroom instruction and behind-the-wheel training.

With your learner's permit in hand, you can start practicing driving under the supervision of a licensed driver. The amount of practice required varies by state, but most require a minimum number of hours behind the wheel.

Once you've completed your driver's education and practice driving, you'll need to pass a road test to obtain your driver's license. This test will assess your ability to drive safely. You'll need to follow the rules of the road.

Many states and countries have a graduated driver's license program, which means that new drivers are subject to certain restrictions until they gain more experience. For example, you may be required to drive with a licensed adult in the car for a certain amount of time, or you may be restricted from driving at night or with passengers under a certain age.

Every few years you'll need to renew your driver's license – it depends what country you live in. You may need to pass a vision test or retake the written or road test to renew your license.

Driving is a serious responsibility, and it's important to prioritize safety on the road at all times.

Car maintenance

Keeping your car well-maintained is essential for ensuring that it runs smoothly and safely. Here are some car maintenance tips to help you keep your car in top condition:

Check your oil regularly

Your car's engine relies on oil to run smoothly, so it's important to check your oil level regularly and change it according to the manufacturer's recommendations.

Keep your tires inflated

Proper tire pressure can improve your gas mileage and help prevent accidents. Check your tire pressure regularly and make sure your tires are inflated to the recommended level.

Change your air filter

A dirty air filter can reduce your car's performance and even cause damage to your engine. Check your air filter regularly and change it as needed.

Keep your car clean

Washing your car is a good idea as it can help prevent rust and damage to the paint. It's also a good idea to clean the inside of your car to prevent dirt and debris from building up.

Check your brakes

Your brakes are one of the most important safety features on your car. Have them checked regularly and replace the brake pads as needed.

Check your fluids

Your car relies on a variety of fluids, including coolant, transmission fluid, and brake fluid. Check your fluid levels regularly and top them off as needed.

Pay attention to warning signs

If your car starts making strange noises or behaving differently than usual, it's important to pay attention to these warning signs and have your car inspected by a mechanic.

International travel & airport tips

Why travel?

Travel can be incredibly beneficial for people of all ages including teenagers, for a variety of reasons. Firstly, it allows people to break out of their routines and experience new things, which can be incredibly refreshing and rejuvenating. It can also provide an opportunity to disconnect from technology and be present in the moment, which can be a great way to reduce stress and increase mindfulness.

Travel can also be amazing for personal growth and education. By navigating new places and cultures, people can learn a lot about themselves and their values. It can also be a chance to challenge oneself and step outside of one's comfort zone, which can be incredibly empowering and confidence-building. Moreover, travel can provide a greater understanding and appreciation of different cultures, customs, and ways of life. It can foster greater empathy and understanding of others.

Finally, travel can simply be a lot of fun! It can create lasting memories and provide a sense of adventure and excitement that can be hard to replicate in daily life.

Reasons to travel

There are so many reasons people love traveling!

To learn a new language

Some people travel abroad to learn a new language or to improve their language skills. This can be a great way to immerse oneself in a new culture and gain a deeper understanding of its people.

To pursue educational opportunities

Some people travel abroad to pursue educational opportunities such as studying abroad, attending conferences or workshops, or participating in cultural exchange programs. In some colleges you can choose to spend a few months or a year studying abroad.

To experience new cultures

Many people travel to foreign countries to immerse themselves in a new culture and learn about its customs, traditions, and history. Backpacking is a type of travel that involves carrying all of one's essential belongings in a backpack and traveling independently or with a small group of people. Backpackers typically travel on a budget and may stay in hostels, campgrounds, or other low-cost accommodations.

Backpacking can be a great way to see the world, meet new people, and experience different cultures. It allows for a lot of flexibility and spontaneity, as backpackers can change their itinerary and plans on the fly. Backpacking can also be a great way to challenge oneself, as it often involves navigating unfamiliar places and situations.

One of the benefits of backpacking is that it can be a very affordable way to travel. By staying in hostels or camping, and cooking meals rather than eating out, backpackers can save a lot of money compared to more traditional forms of travel. Backpacking can also be a great way to connect with other travelers from around the world, as hostels and other low-cost accommodations often attract a diverse group of people. While backpacking can be a lot of fun, it's important to be prepared and take necessary precautions to stay safe. This might include researching the places you plan to visit, carrying appropriate gear and supplies, and being aware of local customs and laws.

To visit family and friends

Many people travel abroad to visit family and friends who live in other countries. People of all ages travel abroad for a variety of reasons, and each trip can offer a unique and rewarding experience.

Apply for a passport

If you're planning to travel internationally, you'll need a valid passport to enter most countries. It's a good idea to apply for a passport asap, even if your trip is several months away.

In general, it's recommended that you apply for a passport at least six months before your planned travel date, as it can take several weeks to receive your passport after submitting your application. However, if you need a passport more quickly, sometimes a fast track option is available.

If you're renewing a passport, you can apply up to a year before it expires. However, keep in mind that some countries say your passport must be valid for at least six months after your planned departure date, so it's important to check the entry requirements for the countries you'll be visiting.

To apply for a passport, you'll need to fill out an application form, provide proof of identity and citizenship, and submit a passport photo.

Packing tips

Here are a few key tips that can help make the process easier and ensure that you have everything you need.

Make a packing list

First make a list of everything you'll need for your trip. This can help you avoid forgetting important items and ensure that you don't over pack.

Pack versatile clothing

Try to pack clothing that can be mixed and matched to create different outfits, and that can be dressed up or down as needed.

Roll your clothes

Rolling your clothes instead of folding them is a handy way to save space in your suitcase and reduce wrinkles.

Pack a travel-size first aid kit

Have a small first aid kit with you when you travel, with essentials like bandages, pain relievers, and any prescription medications you need.

Pack a reusable water bottle

Bringing a reusable water bottle can help you stay hydrated while you travel, and reduce your use of single-use plastic bottles.

Leave some space in your suitcase

It's a good idea to leave some space in your suitcase for souvenirs or other items you may pick up on your trip.

Don't forget important documents

Bring all the necessary documents for your trip, such as your passport, travel itinerary, and any visas or vaccination records required for the countries you'll be visiting.

Remember, pack light and pack smart. With these strategies, you can check that you have everything you need for your trip without over packing or bringing unnecessary items.

Airport tips

Going to the airport can be a bit stressful, especially if you're not a frequent traveler. Here are some airport tips that can help make the process smoother:

Arrive early

Arrive at the airport early, especially if you're traveling during a busy time or to an international destination. Plan to arrive at least two hours before your scheduled departure time.

Check in online

Check in online before your flight, as this can save you time at the airport. Make sure to print your boarding pass or have it saved on your phone.

Pack smart

Make sure to check the latest rules on carrying liquids, gels, and aerosols. Also, make sure to pack any electronics or valuables in your carry-on bag.

Wear comfortable clothing

Wear comfortable clothing and shoes, as you may need to walk long distances or stand in lines for extended periods of time.

Follow security procedures

When going through security, make sure to remove any liquids or electronics from your carry-on bag, take off your shoes and jacket, and place all of your items in a bin to be scanned.

Stay hydrated

Bring an empty water bottle through security. Then fill it up at a water fountain once you're through. Staying hydrated can help you feel better during your flight.

Know your gate

Check the flight information display boards to find your gate number, and give yourself plenty of time to get there.

Relax

Once you're through security and have found your gate, try to relax and enjoy your travel experience. Bring a book, listen to music, or grab a bite to eat before your flight.

Travel hacks

Traveling is an amazing experience, but it can also be stressful and overwhelming at times. Fortunately, there are many travel hacks that can make your trip easier, more efficient, and more enjoyable. Whether you're a pro traveler or off on your first big trip, these tips and tricks can help you save time, money, and hassle. I will share some useful travel hacks that cover everything from packing to navigating airports to staying connected while on the go. These hacks are sure to make your next trip a breeze!

Use a travel app

Download a travel app to help you plan and organize your trip.

Roll your clothes

Rolling your clothes instead of folding them can help save space in your suitcase.

Pack a portable charger

Bring a portable charger for your phone or other electronics so you can stay connected while on the go.

Bring an empty water bottle

Bring an empty water bottle through security and fill it up at a water fountain once you're through. Staying hydrated can help you feel better during your flight.

Pack a scarf

Bring a scarf or shawl that can double as a blanket or pillow on the plane.

Pack a small bag in your carry-on

Pack a small bag in your carry-on with essentials like a change of clothes, toothbrush, and any medications you need in case your checked bag is lost or delayed.

Bring a reusable shopping bag

Bring a reusable shopping bag to use for souvenirs or groceries.

Research local customs

Do some research on the local customs and etiquette before you go to avoid any cultural faux pas.

Bring a photocopy of your passport

Bring a photocopy of your passport and keep it in a separate location from your actual passport. This could be very handy in case it gets lost or stolen.

Book direct flights

Book direct flights whenever possible to avoid layovers and minimize travel time.

Use a VPN

Use a VPN to access your bank accounts or other sensitive information securely while traveling.

Pack snacks

Bring snacks with you to avoid overpriced airport food or to have something to munch on during a long flight.

These travel hacks can help make your trip more efficient, comfortable, and enjoyable.

Conclusion

In conclusion, life skills are essential for teenagers to learn and develop in order to navigate the challenges of adulthood. From managing finances to developing healthy relationships, the skills covered in this book will help teens create a happy, safe and successful life. By mastering these skills, teens can gain the confidence and independence they need to thrive as adults.

I truly hope that reading this book has been really useful and helped you have great success and happiness in life as a teen. You can quickly implement the lessons you learned in your daily life and notice the positive effects.

Before you go, I have a small request to make. I would really appreciate it if you could review this book and share your lessons learned. Doing so will help me a lot in getting this book out to other teens who can benefit from the tips and strategies I have shared.

We only get one chance to live our lives. Dream big and don't have any regrets.

You've got this!

www.ingramcontent.com/pod-product-compliance
Lightning Source LLC
Chambersburg PA
CBHW070948090125
20119CB00011B/592